New Vanguard • 49

Mississippi River Gunboats of the American Civil War 1861–65

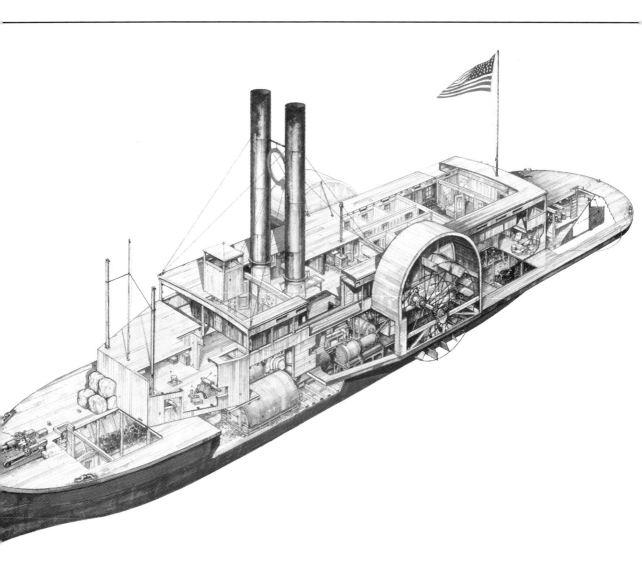

Angus Konstam • Illustrated by Tony Bryan

First published in Great Britain in 2002 by Osprey Publishing, Elms Court, Chapel Way, Botley, Oxford OX2 9LP, United Kingdom.
Email: info@ospreypublishing.com

ISBN 1 84176 413 2

Editor: Simone Drinkwater
Design: Ken Vail Graphic Design, Cambridge, UK
Index by: Alan Rutter
Origination by Grasmere Digital Imaging, Leeds, UK
Printed in China through World Print Ltd.

02 03 04 05 06   10 9 8 7 6 5 4 3 2 1

For a catalogue of all books published by Osprey Military and Aviation please contact:

The Marketing Manager, Osprey Direct UK, PO Box 140, Wellingborough, Northants, NN8 4ZA, United Kingdom.
Tel. +44 (0)1933 443863, Fax +44 (0)1933 443849.
Email: info@ospreydirect.co.uk

The Marketing Manager, Osprey Direct USA,
c/o Motorbooks International, PO Box 1,
Osceola, WI 54020-0001, USA.
Email: info@ospreydirectusa.com

www.ospreypublishing.com

Artist's Note

Readers may care to note that the original paintings from which the colour plates in this book were prepared are available for private sale. All reproduction copyright whatsoever is retained by the Publishers. All enquiries should be addressed to:

Tony Bryan, 4a Forest View Drive, Wimborne, Dorset, BH21 7NZ, UK

The Publishers regret that they can enter into no correspondence upon this matter.

Editor's note

All images are part of the Hensley Collection, Jupiter Beach, Florida, unless otherwise credited.

MISSISSIPPI RIVER GUNBOATS OF THE AMERICAN CIVIL WAR 1861–65

INTRODUCTION

The struggle for the Mississippi River was the longest, most challenging and diverse campaign of the Civil War. It involved the widespread use of ironclads, steam-powered gunboats, modern fortifications, amphibious riverine landings, and the employment of mines. All of these were new, relatively untested instruments of war. Not only would this new form of warfare dominate the struggle for the spine of America, but the struggle would take place on a hitherto unimaginable geographical scale. The river was the natural highway through the continent, and the theater of operations would stretch along it for some 700 miles from Mound City, Illinois, to the Gulf of Mexico. In addition, although the fall of Vicksburg in July 1863 ensured that the Mississippi River itself was cleared of Confederate naval forces, other Southern naval units continued to operate on many of the Mississippi's tributaries. Fighting along these secondary waters would ensure that gunboats of both sides would continue to see service until the end of the war. Although ironclads such as the USS *Cairo* or the CSS *Arkansas* captured the public imagination, the battle for the Mississippi and her tributaries could not have been fought were it not for the dozens of less glamorous wooden gunboats who contested America's inland waterways. This work describes these remarkable little warships.

The Mississippi River port of Memphis, Tennessee, served as the principal naval yard for the Confederate River Defense Fleet on the upper Mississippi. A nascent naval base had been created on the city's riverfront before the war.

THE MISSISSIPPI THEATER

At the outbreak of the Civil War, both sides were largely unprepared for the conflict. This lack of readiness was most apparent in the two navies; the Union fleet was scattered across the globe and the Confederate Navy had not yet come into being. From the start, President Lincoln and his Secretary of the Navy, Gideon Welles, both supported the adoption of a broad strategy, outlined by General Winfield Scott. His strategy, nicknamed "the Anaconda plan," envisioned the blockade and encirclement of the Confederacy by naval forces. A coastal blockade would be augmented by a strike down the Mississippi River from the north, linking up with the ocean-going fleet at New Orleans. By seizing control of the Mississippi River, the Union would be able to split the Confederacy in two. Not only would this starve the heartland of the Confederacy of resources of men and provisions from the western states of Texas, Louisiana, and Arkansas, but it would also reopen the river to Northern trade, a vital prerequisite for economic growth.

The only problem was that the Union had no naval forces on the river which could fulfil these lofty strategic goals. On April 29, 1861, a St Louis businessman called James M. Eads sent a proposal to the Navy Department outlining the facilities available on the Missouri and Illinois shores of the Mississippi River. Although Gideon Welles was fully involved in the establishment of a blockade around the Confederate coast, a dialog involving Eads and both the Army and the Navy resulted in the order to produce a small riverine flotilla. The first of these wooden gunboats entered service in August, at a time when the Confederates were busy constructing their own fleet. The state of Louisiana had purchased a couple of river steamers, and had converted them into gunboats. A second flotilla was earmarked for the defense of the upper Mississippi River, along the Tennessee shore. Similarly, the capture of the Union's Norfolk Navy Base in Virginia ensured the Confederates had access to sufficient guns to defend the river, and several powerful batteries were planned to block Union access to the Mississippi, Cumberland, and Tennessee Rivers. The Confederates were well aware of the importance of the Mississippi River to their survival, and the

The naval yard at Mound City, Illinois, served as a supply and repair base for Union river gunboats. The facilities were basic but, following the transfer of the river fleet from Army to Navy control in August 1862, more extensive floating repair shops were created.

Union strategy. Even if they only held one bastion on the river, or kept one warship afloat, the South would deny the use of the river to the enemy. Both sides braced themselves for a campaign that would be fought over huge distances, and require the close cooperation of both land and naval forces. The challenges facing strategists were daunting.

What emerged was a campaign involving the attack on these Confederate naval and riverside defenses by two fleets: One descending the river from Cairo, Illinois, and the other (after the fall of New Orleans in April 1862) working its way up from the

Union river transports played a vital part in the campaigning along the Mississippi River and its tributaries. This rare photograph is of the river transport *Chickamauga*, operated by the War Department. (National Archives)

Gulf of Mexico. After a brilliantly executed attack on Fort Henry and Fort Donelson on the Tennessee and Cumberland Rivers, Union naval forces in the upper Mississippi faced a series of imposing fortifications. Although the fortifications at Island No. 10 and Fort Pillow were captured by other means, Union wooden gunboats had their chance for glory in two battles at Fort Pillow and Memphis. In these two engagements the Confederate River Defense Fleet was decimated, and only the guns of Vicksburg prevented the entire river falling into Union hands. Even then, Confederate naval units on the Yazoo River caused a near collapse of the Union naval effort before the city of Vicksburg fell to General Grant in July 1863. When Port Hudson fell a week later, the entire Mississippi lay in Union hands, and dozens of wooden gunboats patrolled the hard-won water. Control of tributaries such as the Cumberland and Tennessee Rivers ensured that Union gunboats, transports, and supply boats could travel unimpeded into Tennessee, Kentucky, Mississippi, and upper Alabama. Further to the west, Confederate forces operated on the Red River, and a campaign there would culminate in a humiliating retreat by the Union, and would ensure that Confederate resistance in Arkansas and northern Louisiana would continue until the end of the war.

The gunboats produced by both north and south represented a solution to the strategic and logistical problems which faced the naval commanders of both sides. Both converted and purpose-built wooden gunboats would play their part in this great conflict. Although to most sailors, they were mere "floating wooden bandboxes," these vessels were capable of performing tasks other warships were unable to perform. Like a giant fan, the Mississippi River and its tributaries spread across thousands of miles of the American heartland. The little wooden gunboats of both combatants would reach into virtually every part of this brown-watered arena.

THE UNION RIVER FLEET

The Timberclads

When James B. Eads submitted a proposal to build a flotilla designed to wrest control of the Mississippi River from the Confederates, he was echoing the call by General Winfield Scott to make the river a major focal point of Union strategy. Eads was a successful St Louis businessman, and experienced in riverboat construction. The Navy was hard-pressed just to establish a blockade around the Confederate coastline, so the matter was passed to the War Department, which ran the US Army. What the Navy Department could do was to send an experienced naval officer to supervise operations. In May 1861, Commander John Rodgers, USN, and Naval Constructor Samuel Pook were sent westward, with orders to work with Eads and the theater commander, General McClellan. As the War Department put it:

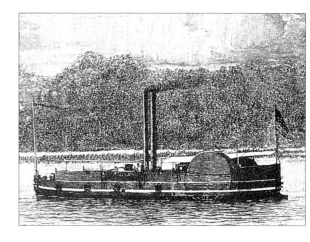

"Mr. James B. Eads, of St Louis, has proposed as a means of defense … the employment of the boats owned by the wrecking company of which he is a member, and has advised that said boats be taken by the Government and properly armed and equipped for that service … It is ordered that the subject be referred to General McClellan, who will consult with Mr. Eads and with such naval officer as the Navy Department may send out for that purpose, and then, as he shall find best, take order for the proper preparation of the boats."

Rodgers was allocated access to naval personnel, but everything else had to be arranged through the Army.

While Rodgers and Eads discussed plans for the creation of an ironclad flotilla, Pook inspected three sidewheel steamers on the Ohio River which Rodgers had selected as potential gunboats for "naval service in these waters." Pook agreed with Rodgers's selection, and on June 8 the US Government duly purchased the *Lexington, Tyler,* and *Conestoga* in Cincinnati for $62,000.

As warships, the trio were less than ideal. Observers dubbed them "bandboxes." Their engines were located above the waterline, and their high sides made them easy targets. Pook supervised their conversion, lowering their engines, reducing their superstructure, and reinforcing their hulls to allow the vessels to carry heavy guns. Oak bulwarks five inches thick protected the gun crews from small arms fire. By the end of June 1861 this initial work had been completed, although Rodgers and Pook criticized the standard of workmanship of the Cincinnati yard which undertook the conversion. As the water level of the Ohio dropped due to seasonal factors, Rodgers ordered the gunboats to be brought down to Cairo, together with the shipyard workers, but they only got as far as Louisville, Kentucky, before they were trapped by the falling waters. Lieutenant Seth L. Phelps arrived in Louisville to take charge of the stranded vessels. Two other officers (Lieutenant Roger Stembe and Master Joshua Bishop) tasked with command of the riverboats began to recruit naval volunteers in Cincinnati. The Army did little to help.

The gunboat USS *Tyler* was the most powerful of the three timberclad gunboats which saw service in the Union river fleet. She can be distinguished from the USS *Lexington* by the midships position of her smokestacks, and from the USS *Conestoga* by her shorter hull.

The timberclad gunboat USS *Lexington* usually operated in conjunction with the USS *Tyler*, and served with distinction throughout the war. She is probably best remembered for providing naval gunfire support to General Grant's Union Army at the Battle of Shiloh in April 1862.

Meanwhile, McClellan had been replaced by General Fremont, and the new regional commander asked for Rodgers's removal, due to the complaints of local businessmen that he was not displaying enough largesse with naval contracts. The capable Rodgers was duly sent back east.

At Louisville, Phelps struggled to complete the gunboats. Phelps complained "there is no paint for the boats," and questioned the quality of the rivermen hired by his colleagues. Finally, the river rose enough for the three gunboats to continue on to Cairo, where their guns and stores waited for them on the quayside. The trio constituted the only river defense available to the Union, and were duly put to work by the Army. While they were crewed by Navy personnel, they (and all other Union river gunboats) came under Army control. The river flotilla would only be transferred to the US Navy in August 1862. They were available for service by August 15, 1861, and six days later the *Tyler* fired the first naval "shot in anger" on the Mississippi, engaging Confederate patrols on the Missouri shore. The trio would operate in support of the Army until enough warships were gathered to permit independent naval operations.

These wooden gunboats were only protected by timber. With a touch of sarcasm, in comparison with the ironclads designed by Eads and Pook, they were duly dubbed "timberclads." Despite their fragile appearance, they were useful, well-armed warships. The *Conestoga* only carried four

The timberclad gunboat USS *Conestoga* first saw service in September 1861, and subsequently took part in the attacks on Fort Henry and Fort Donelson. She was sunk in a collision with the USS *General Price* in March 1864.

32-pounders, but her consorts were stronger, allowing the emplacement of a heavier broadside armament. The *Lexington* carried two 32-pounder, and four 8-inch smoothbores, while the *Tyler* carried one 32-pounder and six 8-inch smoothbore pieces. Although all these weapons were smoothbores, changes were made to these ordnance suites during the war. The *Lexington* and *Tyler* were issued with 30-pounder rifles by late 1862 (two and three respectively) but the

Conestoga was not similarly up-gunned. The effectiveness of rifled guns against shore positions had been demonstrated on both the Mississippi and the Eastern seaboard, so this re-equipping reflected a change in the perceived role of the gunboats, from vessels designed to fight other warships to ones capable of suppressing fire from Confederate shore positions.

The Rams

In 1861 Charles Rivers Ellet, Jr., was a civil engineer with experience in the building of bridges and dams. During the Crimean War (1854–56), he traveled to Russia as an observer, and had become convinced that the ram used by the warships of antiquity could be adapted. By using steam power, it could become a viable modern naval weapon. He convinced the Union War Department of the worth of his idea and, in early 1862, he was made a colonel, with orders to create a ram flotilla, which would join the timberclads on the Mississippi. During April he purchased nine vessels, both sidewheelers and sternwheelers, at various ports on the Ohio River, and began the work of converting them into warships. This work took place in several yards: the *Queen of the West* and *Lancaster* were converted in Cincinnati, Ohio, the *Switzerland* in Madison, Indiana, the *Monarch* in New Albany, Indiana, and the *Mingo, Lioness,* and *Sampson* in Pittsburgh, Pennsylvania. When they became ready for final fitting out they were taken to New Albany or Mound City for completion. Another ram, the *T.D. Horner,* was deemed unsuitable, and used as a tug instead, while a ninth vessel was used as transport.

These vessels varied in size, appearance, and propulsion system, but all shared two characteristics. They were designed primarily as rams, and they were commanded by Colonel Ellet, whose enthusiasm for ram tactics had led to their creation. They mostly possessed little in the way of armament (usually one or two 12-pounder howitzers or 24-pounder smoothbores), but they had their bows reinforced by timber, and their hulls strengthened to absorb the shock of a collision. They were also faster than the timberclads, having an average speed of 12 knots. On May 26, 1862, the first of these ships joined the timberclads above Fort Pillow. Although an independent unit, the ram flotilla formed part of the Western Gunboat Flotilla, as the timberclads were now designated. When the rest of the river fleet came under the control of the US Navy in August 1862, the rams remained under orders of the War Department. Some critics considered them to be "brown paper rams," but Ellet's vessels would demonstrate their worth in action.

Although the need for the rams passed, as Confederate naval forces were swept from the Mississippi, the notion of the ram as a weapon remained in vogue. Two other rams were built for the War Department during 1863 and on

Colonel Charles Ellet was a staunch advocate of the wooden ram, and his flotilla of "Ellet rams" helped turn the tide of the war on the upper Mississippi River. He was mortally wounded at the Battle of Memphis in June 1862.

The late-war ram USS *Vindicator* photographed moored to a riverbank on the Mississippi in late 1864. She fought the CSS *Webb* when the Confederate ram made a dash from the Red River down the Mississippi in April 1865. (US Navy)

completion they were transferred to the Navy. The first of these to enter service was the *Avenger*, built in New Albany, Indiana, and completed in February 1864. Three months later the same yard completed the gunboat *Vindicator*, which was duly taken to Mound City and converted into a ram. Both joined the Mississippi Squadron in the summer of 1864, and participated in patrols around Vicksburg, and on the Yazoo River. They were not particularly successful, although they were formidable gunboats, combining their ram with a powerful armament, including a 100-pounder Parrott bow rifle mounted in a wooden casemate. The *Vindicator* engaged the Confederate ram *Webb* off the mouth of the Red River in April 1865, but otherwise they saw no active service.

After 1862, clashes with Confederate warships were almost unknown, and the rams became less useful. While the *Queen of the West* carried a respectable armament of four guns (accounts vary, but the most probable suite was one 20- or 30-pounder Parrott rifle and three 12-pounder howitzers), other rams had a limited armament. The *Switzerland* was converted into a gunboat in late 1862 and, although her exact armament is unknown, photographs and sketches suggest she carried eight guns, probably a mixed suite of 12-pounder howitzers and 24-pounder rifles or smoothbores, split between two broadsides. As other rams were used in shore bombardments from late 1862 on, it seems probable that the remaining ships of Ellet's fleet were converted shortly after they were transferred into naval service in August 1862. These fast, useful vessels clearly had their role redefined as the war progressed, although they still retained their ramming capability.

Tinclads

It soon became apparent that the Union needed more than a few powerful ironclads and rams on the Mississippi. While the principal units of the River Flotilla were occupied in the seizure or bombardment of Confederate shore positions or the destruction of enemy warships, other river gunboats were needed to patrol the hundreds of miles of rivers which led through occupied territory. Their roles were to escort supply boats and troop transports, to patrol for signs of enemy activity, or to act as dispatch boats, linking the Union armies in the Western Theater with their depots and recruiting bases further north. For this purpose dozens of flat-bottomed river steamers were purchased and converted into warships. Although many were propelled by sidewheel propulsion, the majority were sternwheelers, similar to or smaller than the craft made famous as Mississippi "gambling" boats (more accurately they were passenger ferries). To protect them from enemy small arms fire from the shore, these vessels were lightly armored with thin metal sheeting. This

LEFT **The Ellet ram USS *Switzerland* was an ungainly, slab-sided vessel, but her roomy casemate permitted the addition of extra armament following the destruction of the Confederate River Defense Fleet in June 1862.**

The Union timberclad gunboats **USS *Lexington*** and **USS *Tyler*** engaging Confederate shore batteries at Columbus, Kentucky, in January 1862. These small but powerful vessels probably saw more service than any other gunboats in the Western Theater.

The USS *Ouachita* was the largest and best-armed tinclad gunboat on the Mississippi, carrying almost 40 guns, including five 30-pounder Parrott rifles. She participated in the capture of the Confederate ironclad CSS *Missouri* on the Red River in June 1865.

gave rise to the name "tinclad." From June 19, 1863 (just before the fall of Vicksburg), apart from the two largest vessels, these tinclads were allocated identification numbers, which were painted on the sides of the vessels' pilot houses.

The largest of these tinclads served as a Command Ship for acting Rear Admiral David Dixon Porter, who had assumed command of Union river forces in September 1862. The *Black Hawk* was built in New Albany, Indiana, in 1848, and began life as a luxury paddle steamer called the *New Uncle Sam*. She was purchased by the Navy Department for $36,000 in November 1862, and although she was theoretically converted into a gunboat, she retained many of her luxurious internal fittings. She joined the fleet on December 6, 1862, above Vicksburg, and served as the Union command vessel on both the Mississippi and Red Rivers until she was destroyed by an accidental fire off Cairo, Illinois, in April 1865. She carried two 32-pounder smoothbores, two 30-pounder Parrott rifles, and two 12-pounder pieces, but she only fired her guns in anger once, during an attack on Haynes' Bluff, Mississippi, in late April 1863. The large stately flagship was too valuable a vessel to risk in action.

The second large un-numbered tinclad was the *Ouachita*, a former Confederate steamer called the *Louisville,* which was captured on a tributary of the Red River in July 1863. She was duly converted into a gunboat, and entered service on January 18, 1864 in time to participate in the Red River Campaign. She carried five 30-pounder Parrott rifles and eighteen 24-pounder and fifteen 12-pounder smoothbores, making her the most powerful gunboat in the Western Theater.

These two vessels were the exception. Most of the other 69 tinclads to enter service displaced less than 200 tons, and were armed with far less

impressive suites of ordnance. Almost all carried between four and eight guns, a mixture of whatever was available, although rifled guns were introduced as they were produced. In all but one case, the largest guns carried were 30-pounder rifles or 32-pounder smoothbores, although 20-pounder rifles, 24-pounder smoothbores and 12-pounders of both types were far more common.

The exception was the USS *James Thompson* (renamed *Manitou*, then *Fort Hindman* in late 1863) which was 150 feet long and displaced 280 tons. She was purchased by the Navy Department at Jeffersonville, Indiana, in March 1863, and entered service just weeks later, after having strips of tin nailed around her superstructure and paddlewheel boxes. She carried an unusually heavy armament of two 8-inch smoothbores in her bow, with two more on each broadside.

The USS *Marmora* (No. 2) was a more typical tinclad. She was built in Monongahela, Pennsylvania, then sold to the Navy Department in September 1862. She was 155 feet long and displaced 207 tons. Her twin engines and boilers powered a sternwheel that was capable of propelling the ship at just under 7 knots. She was armed with two 24-pounder and two 12-pounder rifles arranged in broadsides in her tinclad casemate, although four more 24-pounders were added in mid-1864. She entered service in October 1862, and participated in expeditions up the Yazoo and White Rivers during a distinguished wartime career, which also involved attacks on the defenses of Vicksburg and Fort Hindman.

All in all these tinclad river gunboats were ungainly, slow and unprepossessing, but without them the Union would never have managed to supply its field armies in the West, or keep them in communication with each other.

Other Union gunboats and service craft

In addition to these main gunboat types, the US Navy and the War Department operated a number of other vessels on the Mississippi and its tributaries. Some of these, such as the USS *General Bragg* or the USS *Sumter*, were gunboats captured from the Confederates. Others performed non-combatant roles. Several captured Confederate vessels

The powerful tinclad USS *Fort Hindman* (No. 13) had her name changed several times, being commissioned as the USS *James Thompson*. Her name was altered to celebrate the capture of the Confederate fort guarding the Arkansas River. (US Navy)

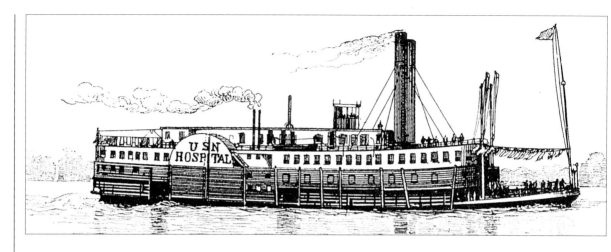

The US Navy's first hospital ship was the USS *Red Rover*, a former Confederate river steamer which was captured at Island No. 10 in April 1862. She carried a medical staff of 30 doctors and nurses, and had facilities for the treatment of over 200 casualties. (US Navy)

were used as storeships or ordnance boats, while other support craft were purchased by the War Department. These vessels included the 625-ton USS *Red Rover*, the US Navy's first hospital ship. Around a dozen tugs were attached to the river fleet, and these were frequently called on to guide the larger warships through narrow tributaries, or to pull them off sandbars. Although the tugs were unarmed, other support craft occasionally carried a minimal armament of 12-pounders or sometimes larger pieces. Their role was strictly a supporting one, and these guns were purely provided for self-defense.

THE CONFEDERATE RIVER FLEET

The New Orleans Squadron

In the summer and fall of 1861 shipyards in and around New Orleans converted or laid down a small flotilla of warships, both wooden gunboats and ironclads. These included two floating batteries, three ironclads and numerous river gunboats, or converted ocean-going steamers. A fleet of 10 wooden warships (including three tugs) was ready to contest the attack on the defenses below New Orleans by Commodore David G. Farragut's Western Gulf Blockading Squadron on April 24, 1862. In addition, two ironclads were available, although one, the *Louisiana*, was still unfinished, and needed to be towed into position. The sidewheel gunboat CSS *Jackson* was absent from the fleet when the Union attacked, and the remainder constituted the core of the naval defenses of New Orleans. Political control of this flotilla was a complete mess. Two gunboats, the CSS *McRae* and the CSS *Jackson* belonged to the regular Confederate Navy, as did the ironclads CSS *Manassas* and *Louisiana* and a handful of tugs

The *Governor Moore* pictured after the fight with the USS *Varuna* below New Orleans, moments before the crew abandoned ship and her commander set her on fire. She was not officially a Confederate naval vessel as she remained part of the Louisiana Provisional Navy until her destruction.

and tenders. The cottonclad rams *Governor Moore* and *General Quitman* were operated by the Louisiana State Navy rather than the Confederate government, while six other cottonclad gunboats or rams belonged to the River Defense Fleet, run by the Confederate Army (*Defiance*, *General Breckenridge*, *General Lovell*, *Resolute*, *Warrior*, and *Stonewall Jackson*). Neither group was willing to take orders from the Navy, and all three existed as separate administrative and tactical entities.

The *McRae* was a former Mexican steamer which had been seized for piracy in 1860. She was still impounded in New Orleans when Louisiana seceded from the Union. The long, sleek, bark-rigged gunboat was powered by a single screw, and armed with a 9-inch Dahlgren smoothbore on a central pivot mounting, in addition to a regular broadside armament of six 32-pounders and a 12-pounder. By contrast the *Stonewall Jackson* was armed with a single gun, mounted on her quarterdeck. Her primary armament was a ram, and during the Battle of New Orleans in April 1862 its effectiveness was demonstrated when the vessel rammed and sank the gunboat USS *Varuna*. The *Governor Moore* was also a ram, and she struck the *Varuna* herself, but with little effect. Even more spectacularly, in order to keep firing when the two ships were locked together, the crew of the 32-pounder on her forecastle fired through their own deck in order to hit the *Varuna* below her waterline. Both the *Governor Moore* and the *Stonewall Jackson* were sunk during the battle. The second Louisiana vessel, the *General Quitman*, was a ram, but it failed to hit any Union target.

As for the appearance of these vessels, Captain Beverley Kennon, the commander of the *Governor Moore*, provided a detailed description.

"The vessel which I commanded was formerly the ocean-built wooden paddle-steamship Charles Morgan *of about 900 tons and having a walking-beam engine. When armed by the State of Louisiana she was named the* Governor Moore, *and received 2 rifled 32-pounders (not banded and not sighted), and a complement of 93 persons. She was not iron-plated in any manner whatever. Her stem was like that of hundreds of other vessels, being faced its length on its edges above water with two strips of old-fashioned flat railroad iron, held in place by short straps of like kind at the top, at the waterline, and at three intermediate points. These straps extended about two feet abaft the face of the stem on each side, where they were bolted in place. The other 'rams' had their 'noses' hardened in like manner. All had the usual-shaped stems. Not one had an iron beak or projecting prow under the water. All of them had their boiler-houses, engines, and boilers protected by a bulkhead of cotton bales which extended from the floor of the hold to about five feet or more above the spar deck. These and other such*

Union sharpshooters from the 75th New York Regiment picking off the gunners of a Confederate gunboat on a Louisiana river in January 1863. Ambushes from the shore were a frequent occurrence on the Mississippi River and her tributaries throughout the war.

The elegant screw gunboat CSS *McRae* was formerly a warship in the Mexican Navy, and was bought into Confederate service in 1861. She operated in the Mississippi Delta until her destruction at the Battle of New Orleans in April 1862.

vessels were fitted out by the State and the city of New Orleans after the regular navy neglected to take them, and to Lieutenant-Colonel W.S. Lovell (ex-lieutenant United States Navy) is due the credit of their novel construction.

"Of the remaining seven 'rams' the General Quitman *was like my ship, but smaller. The remaining six had been tug-boats, and were of wood, with walking-beam engines. Each of them mounted one or two guns, had about 35 men, and measured not far from 150 tons. These six 'rams' were an independent command, and recognized no outside authority unless it suited their convenience; and it was expected that this 'fleet' and its branch in Memphis would defend the upper and lower Mississippi, without aid from the regular navy."*

The River Defense Fleet

Initially, a small flotilla, consisting of the gunboats *Livingston*, *General Polk*, *Pontchartrain* and *Maurepas*, was available for service and was stationed at Island No. 10. These four gunboats were all sidewheelers, and displaced between 390 and 460 tons each. Three were built in New Albany, Indiana, and purchased into service in New Orleans in 1861, while the *Livingston* was originally designed as a towboat, but was purchased while still being built in New Orleans, and she was completed as a gunboat. The *General Polk* was a long, sleek vessel, but only carried three 32-pounder guns, two of which were rifled. The remaining three vessels were shorter, stockier, and slower, but carried a larger armament, six to eight guns, including at least two 32-pounder rifles per vessel. Three of them were destroyed to prevent their capture after the fall of Memphis in June 1863, but the *Pontchartrain* continued to operate on the Red River until her destruction in turn in October 1863.

Until March 1862 the flotilla was augmented by the Confederate naval vessels *McRae* and *Jackson* (described above), but these returned south to defend New Orleans when Union forces threatened the city.

The floating battery *New Orleans* also assisted the naval flotilla at Island No. 10. It was immobile, and had to be towed into place, then moored. Consequently, when the land defenses were flanked, the naval flotilla escaped downriver, but the *New Orleans* had to be destroyed to prevent her capture.

While this small flotilla was operating around Island No. 10, a second force was being converted in yards in and around New Orleans. Like their counterparts in the New Orleans Squadron, this Confederate River Defense Fleet was operated by the War Department, and charged with the defense of the upper stretches of the Mississippi, while the southern contingent remained around New Orleans. This force, which took part in the defense of Fort Pillow and the Battle of Memphis (June 6, 1862), centered around a force of eight river steamers, most of which were converted into rams. Under the command of Captain J.E. Montgomery,

whose flagship was the *Little Rebel*, the eight-vessel fleet consisted of the *General Bragg*, *General Sterling Price*, *General Sumter*, *General Earl Van Dorn*, *General M. Jeff Thompson*, *Colonel Lovell* and *General Beauregard*. When the four light gunboats retired from Island No. 10, this fleet constituted the only effective naval force on the upper stretches of the Mississippi, between Cairo and Memphis.

The largest of these ships was the CSS *General Bragg*, formerly a brig-rigged paddlewheel passenger steamer called the *Mexico,* which had operated in the Gulf of Mexico. She was built in New York in 1850 for the Southern Steamship Company, based in New Orleans, and was purchased by the Confederate government in January 1862. A four-inch oak beam was added to her bow, then covered in a one-inch layer of iron, making a rudimentary ram. As the vessel displaced over 1,000 tons and could attain a speed of over 10 knots, she was a powerful ramming vessel. In addition to her ram, she was fitted with a 30-pounder Parrott rifle on her forecastle, and a 32-pounder smoothbore on her quarterdeck.

Of the other seven vessels in the fleet, the *General Sterling Price*, the *General Sumter,* and the *Colonel Lovell* all displaced over 500 tons. The *General Sterling Price* was formerly the *Laurent Millaudon*, a sidewheel riverboat built in Cincinnati, Ohio, in 1856. Apart from her ram, she was armed with four guns, one on the forecastle, another on the quarterdeck, and two in broadside mounts inside her wooden casemate. All were 9-inch Dahlgren smoothbores, making her one of the best-armed wooden vessels on the river.

Almost as powerful was the *General Beauregard* (formerly the New Orleans towboat *Ocean*), which carried four 8-inch and one 42-pounder smoothbore guns. By contrast, the *General Sumter* (once the New Orleans towboat *Junius Beebe*) carried four 32-pounder and one 12-pounder smoothbores. Both the Cincinnati-built steamer *Colonel Lovell* and the former towboat *General Earl Van Dorn* were armed with a single smoothbore gun, mounted on their forecastles. The armament of the *M. Jeff Thompson* was most probably a single bow gun, and the *Little Rebel* (formerly the Pennsylvania screw steamer *R. & J. Watson*) carried three 12-pounder rifles.

The Confederate cottonclad ram *Stonewall Jackson* as she looked before the Battle of New Orleans. A wall of cotton bales protected her, reaching from her keel to above the top of her superstructure.

The cottonclad ram CSS *General Sterling Price* was one of the Confederate River Defense Fleet which fought at Plum Point and Memphis in 1862. Although she was sunk in the Battle of Memphis in June 1862, she was raised, repaired, and operated by the US Navy as the gunboat USS *General Price*. This photograph was taken when she was in Union service.

The CSS *General Bragg* was the largest vessel in the Confederate River Defense Fleet. Although she was sunk at the Battle of Memphis, she was raised and served against her former owners. In this photograph taken in Mound City, Illinois, she is being repaired before entering Union service. (US Navy)

With their varied armament these vessels were little match for the Union river ironclads which opposed them, but they were fast, capable of speeds of 8–10 knots, and they were fitted with crude rams. Apart from the modifications to their bows and the addition of ordnance, they were further protected by the creation of extra bulkheads around their machinery and gundecks, and cotton was compressed into the space between the sides of the superstructure and a false inner bulkhead (like a wood and cotton sandwich) creating a basic form of cottonclad protection. Additional bales were probably stacked around their exposed guns and around their pilot houses.

Following the destruction of the Confederate gunboat flotillas at New Orleans and Memphis, only one other wooden Confederate gunboat caused serious problems for the Union. In January 1863, Colonel W.S. Lovell, the creator of the ram fleet was sent to Alexandria, Louisiana, to convert the riverboat *Webb* into a warship. This wooden sidewheeler had been built in New York in 1856, and was being converted into a privateer in New Orleans when the city fell to the Union. The *Webb* escaped to the Red River. Lovell gave her a ram bow, and placed a 130-pounder James rifle on her forecastle. She was also equipped with two 12-pounder howitzers, as anti-personnel weapons. Cotton bales were stacked around her machinery, so that only her beam engine remained unprotected. The CSS *Webb* performed well in an engagement with the ironclad USS *Indianola*, and ended her career in a dramatic charge down the Mississippi in the last days of the war.

THE ROLE OF GUNBOATS

Function

Strategically, the Union was committed to the opening up of the Mississippi River, from Cairo, Illinois, to the Gulf of Mexico. This could not be achieved by naval forces alone, as troops had to seize and hold the key points along the river, then use these sites to launch attacks which would drive the Confederate armies eastwards away from the Mississippi river. By gaining access to the tributaries of the Mississippi and Ohio rivers, Union forces could strike deep into Confederate territory, and support armies operating in the heartland of the South. The Tennessee and Cumberland Rivers were vital arteries of war and commerce, and the side that controlled them could dominate Kentucky and much of Tennessee.

Following the fall of Fort Henry, which guarded the Tennessee River, Confederate General Johnston wrote that the loss of the fort gave the Union "control of the navigation on the Tennessee River, and their gunboats are now descending … " He argued that the loss of Fort

Donelson would "open the route to the enemy to Nashville, giving them the means of breaking bridges and destroying the ferry boats on the river as far as navigable." His prediction was correct, and after losing both forts, the Confederates were forced to withdraw to the south. The Confederates lacked the gunboats which might have been able to contest control of the two rivers, and consequently, they were forced to pull back behind the two rivers, giving up Kentucky. Similarly, control of the Mississippi and its tributaries allowed Union generals to move troops deep into the Confederate heartland, and to supply these forces from the bustling industrial cities of the Midwest. Without gunboats, the Confederacy lay wide open to the enemy.

Both sides realized that, but the capture of Forts Henry and Donelson took the Confederates by surprise, before they were able to build up the flotillas they needed to defend the Tennessee and Cumberland Rivers. From that point, Union gunboats had two roles, a primarily offensive one, involving the defeat of enemy forces on the Mississippi River, and a secondary defensive one, defending the Tennessee and Cumberland, protecting supply lines, and denying access to the region to the enemy.

Offensive operations usually involved the river ironclads, supported first by the three timberclads, and later by the Ellet ram fleet. As numbers were augmented by tinclad gunboats and captured Confederate vessels, an increasing number of gunboats were allocated a defensive role. Confederate measures involved a limited use of gunboats after the fall of Memphis and, instead, they concentrated on holding key defensive positions on the Mississippi River and its tributaries. Clearly the principal river fortresses were Vicksburg and Port Hudson, but the Red River was also developed as a stronghold and, despite the abortive 1864 campaign, it remained in Confederate hands until the last days of the war.

Initially, both sides built wooden rams, but following the destruction of the Confederate fleets at Memphis and New Orleans, the Union changed their role. Initially, the rams were pure naval vessels designed to fight enemy warships. After Memphis, they became vessels whose primary function was to patrol rivers, and to bombard enemy-held shorelines. The tinclads, which were converted into warships and entered service from 1862 on, were primarily designed for exactly this kind of role. They patrolled rivers, reaching anywhere their shallow drafts could take them. They guarded river crossings, scouted for signs of enemy raiders, escorted transport and supply vessels, carried dispatches, provided gunfire support to operations close to the shore, and bombarded enemy positions. They dragged rivers for torpedoes (as mines were then known), they cleared rivers of obstructions, and they provided a cordon of

Union river gunboats engaging shore targets on the western rivers. Attacks on enemy patrols, naval gunfire support, and the bombardment of shore positions were all regular tasks for the gunboat fleet.

protection for support vessels. In short they were the workhorses of the Western Theater, operating everywhere they were needed, and performing a range of duties. When Confederate guerrillas raided into Indiana and Illinois, gunboats led the pursuit, and helped to contain the raiders. Although larger, more impressive warships such as the ironclads or Confederate ocean raiders, gained the glory, these simple wooden gunboats helped win the war for the Union.

Manpower

Before the war, the Mississippi River and its tributaries made up a bustling system of waterways, linking river ports as far north as Minneapolis, Minnesota, and Pittsburgh, Pennsylvania, with thriving markets downstream. The Missouri River branched westwards through Kansas, while other tributaries covered much of the Southern states which bordered the great river. Within days of the sucession of Tennessee, Arkansas, Mississippi, and Louisiana, access south of the Kentucky state line was denied to the Northern states, and the thriving river trade was brought to an abrupt standstill. In theory, this meant there should have been a rich pool of experienced rivermen for both sides to recruit from. In practice, this was far from the case.

At first, the crews of both sides were a strange mixture of rivermen, soldiers, civilian volunteers, and professional sailors. River pilots were at a premium, and while many had an intimate knowledge of portions of the river network, few knew more than a limited stretch of the river. These men were invaluable, and if captured, financial incentives were usually offered to encourage a change of allegiance.

For the Confederates, manpower was always a problem. By the time the first gunboat fleets were ready for service, most rivermen and mechanics were already serving in the Confederate Army, and very few Army officers were willing to part with men under their command, however eligible they might be for naval rather than land service. Throughout the war on the rivers most Confederate ships were undermanned. There was also a shortage of trained seamen in the South, both in the seaboard ports and on the Mississippi. When the Army was ordered to send drafts of men for naval service, it frequently kept the trained rivermen, and instead used the demand to get rid of the most undesirable or incompetent elements in its commands.

A naval recruiting station (known as a Naval Rendezvous) was established in New Orleans, run by a staff of three officers. Newspaper advertisements, flyers, and recruiting drives were used to encourage volunteers, while officers continually pleaded with their Army counterparts for men. Confederate Marine recruitment offices were also opened in Memphis and New Orleans during 1861. The loss of the two cities meant that,

Lieutenant Thomas B. Huger, CSN, was one of the few regular Confederate naval officers to serve in the Western Theater during the war. He commanded the gunboat CSS *McRae* during the Battle of New Orleans in April 1864.

after mid-1862, most recruits for Confederate gunboats were recruited locally, usually from drafts of state troops or local garrisons.

The Union river fleets were more fortunate, having access to the bustling river ports of Cincinnati, St Louis, or Pittsburgh. Naval Rendezvous offices were set up in all these cities, and from the outset rivermen were encouraged to serve in the flotillas rather than to sign up for service in the Army.

Union officers photographed while off duty. The officer (The Ship's Master) in the center is shown carrying a hunting rifle and accompanied by two hunting dogs. Hunting along the shore was a popular activity when the opportunity presented itself.

Until August 1862 the Union river fleet was run by the War Department, so rivermen were drafted from regular military service to the river fleet. Officers were provided from the regular US Navy, and when the Navy Department took over responsibility for the ships in August 1862, their crews simply switched from one service to another. In addition to the officers, a small proportion of experienced naval ratings and petty officers provided a core of naval experience, and ensured some link with the procedures, drill, regulations, and discipline enforced in the ocean-going fleet. Somehow this mixture of soldiers, sailors, rivermen, and volunteers developed into an effective team, and by 1863 the Union sailors of the brown-water navy had become an experienced and well-trained fighting force.

Ordnance

There was no typical armament for a Mississippi River gunboat during the war. While many were armed with large smoothbore weapons such as 24-pounders and 32-pounders, rifled guns were also widely used, as were small howitzers. Occasionally, some gunboats carried larger pieces, such as the 130-pounder rifle.

In 1845 the US Navy had adopted the 32-pounder smoothbore as its standard gun type, designed to augment larger "shell" guns (64-pounder, 8-inch pieces, introduced in limited numbers in 1841) or regular "solid shot" guns (also 64-pounder pieces). Even as late as the Civil War, many naval officers considered the shell gun a poor substitute for the ship-smashing capabilities of a solid roundshot. Its range was approximately three-quarters of that of an equivalent solid shot, and although it was capable of causing more damage, and of causing fires, it was considered less accurate than a conventional solid projectile.

Perhaps the most common pieces of ordnance carried on river gunboats were bronze 24-pounder and 32-pounder smoothbores. Classified as Model 1841 pieces under the US Army's Mordecai system, the US Navy had a bewildering range of gun types, as 27, 33, 42, 51, 57 and 61-hundredweight versions of the 32-pounder were used by the US Navy. Of these, the last was the most widely used, as many of the earlier, smaller pieces were eventually converted into rifled weapons. Almost as common as the 32-pounder smoothbore was the 24-pounder howitzer, another 1841 pattern piece, whose short length made it an ideal close-range naval weapon.

Recruitment into the Union Navy took place at Naval Rendezvous offices, such as this one in New York City. Similar offices were established in the major river ports, such as Cincinnati, St Louis, and Pittsburgh. Illustration from *Leslie's Illustrated Newspaper*, 1861. (Author's Collection)

The smoothbore shell guns introduced into US Naval service by John A. Dahlgren from 1850 onward began to change this, as his pieces matched conventional guns in both range and accuracy. Although rarely seen on the Mississippi River unless carried on the ocean-going warships of the regular Navy, Dahlgren pieces exerted their own influence over other, earlier forms of ordnance. Standard long guns (conventional smoothbore pieces) were adapted to fire shell as well as solid shot, and a handful of his 8-inch and 32-pounder guns appeared on larger Union gunboats.

A second modification to earlier guns was the conversion of smoothbore guns into rifled pieces. General Charles T. James pioneered this conversion process, which involved the cutting of narrow, deep grooves into the bores of older bronze guns. As the new rifled projectiles weighed approximately twice that of the original solid shot used by the cannon, gun designations were doubled. Consequently, a 6-pounder became a 12-pounder and so on. The largest James rifle found on Mississippi gunboats was the 130-pounder, converted from a 64-pounder smoothbore, and carried on the wooden ram CSS *Webb*. In general, most Confederate rifled pieces were James rifles, while the Union had a plentiful supply of the more efficient Parrott pieces, and these were widely used in the river fleet.

Robert P. Parrott had introduced his own design of iron rifled ordnance for naval service in 1861. The 20-pounder and 30-pounder rifled pieces were commonly found on Union gunboats from 1862 onwards. Compared to smoothbore guns, rifled pieces had a longer range and greater accuracy, but lacked the destructive power of the smoothbore shot or shell, at least against unarmored targets. By contrast, rifled guns mounted in fortifications could hit and penetrate the ironclad fleet used by the Union on the Mississippi, and could disable a wooden gunboat at long range with a single shot.

The following list contains some of the more common guns mounted on wooden gunboats of both sides which operated on the Mississippi River and its tributaries. In fact, such a wide range of pieces was employed that a full listing is beyond the scope of this book. The ranges given are those for the effective range of the pieces, firing solid shot, at an elevation of 5 degrees. Extreme range was often double this, and the maximum effective range for guns firing shell was usually 75–85 percent of the range for solid shot projectiles.

Smoothbore Gun

	Bore	Gun Weight	Gun Length	Construction	Effective Range
12-pounder (1841 pattern)	4⅗ in	1,757 pounds	7ft 6in	Bronze	1,663 yards
24-pounder (1841 pattern)	5⅕ in	6,240 pounds	10ft 4in	Bronze	1,901 yards
32-pounder (1841 pattern)	6⅖ in	6,832 pounds	10ft 5in	Bronze	1,922 yards
8-inch (Columbiad)	8 in	9,210 pounds	10ft 4in	Iron	1,814 yards
9-inch (Dahlgren)	9 in	9,000 pounds	9ft	Iron	2,100 yards

The crew of a 9-inch Dahlgren smoothbore gun operating their piece during a gunnery drill on a gunboat. Although only a few Mississippi river gunboats had guns of this size, the firing drill remained the same. (US Navy)

Rifled Guns

	Bore	Gun Weight	Gun Length	Construction	Effective Range
9–pounder (Rodman)	3in	820 pounds	5ft 9in	Bronze	1,830 yards
10-pounder (Parrott)	3in	890 pounds	6ft 2in	Iron	1,850 yards
12-pounder (James)	3⅔in	875 pounds	5ft	Bronze	1,700 yards
20-pounder (Parrott)	3⅔in	1,750 pounds	7ft	Iron	1,900 yards
30-pounder (Parrott)	4⅓in	4,200 pounds	11ft 4in	Iron	2,200 yards
130-pounder (James)	8½in	14,896 pounds	10ft 10in	Bronze	2,430 yards

Howitzers

	Bore	Gun Weight	Gun Length	Construction	Effective Range
12-pounder (1841 pattern)	4⅔in	788 pounds	4ft 5in	Bronze	1,072 yards
24-pounder (1841 pattern)	5⅛in	1,318 pounds	5ft 5in	Bronze	1,322 yards

Life on Board

In both the Union and Confederate fleets, conditions on board the wooden gunboats that operated on the Mississippi River were better than those found on the cramped river ironclads, or even the crowded decks of the Union ocean-going steam fleet. Even when the first timberclads of the Union fleet or the independent ram flotillas of the Confederates were brought into service, despite their ownership, the crews were organized along naval lines. A smattering of experienced naval officers and petty officers provided enough influence for these vessels to be run the Navy way, although the levels of discipline and "spit-and-polish" would rarely have impressed senior naval officers. Later, as Admiral Foote brought the Union river fleet under his control, a more exacting level of naval authority and discipline was introduced into the river fleets. By the end of the war, these vessels were operated in virtually the same way as all other elements of the US Navy.

Both sides based their daily routines and fighting practices upon those of the prewar US Navy, and therefore there was little or no difference between the running of vessels of the two sides. The one exception was that the Confederates operated a number of semi-independent state squadrons or River Defense Fleets, and although regular naval practices were adopted, the commanders of these vessels operated outside the authority of the regular Confederate Navy. In effect, these units owed their allegiance to their own flotilla commander, not to any naval officer appointed by the Confederate Navy Department. Consequently, while regular warships were supplied and paid by the Navy Department, these units organized their own provisions.

A slightly less divisive situation existed in the Union fleet, where the War Department ran river operations until August 1862, but the vessels themselves were usually crewed by regular naval officers, and their multifarious crews of sailors, soldiers, and rivermen operated under the constraints of naval discipline. Following the take-over of the river fleets by the US Navy, these divisions were overcome, and the fleet developed into a unified naval force.

Most gunboats operated from established bases: New Orleans, Memphis, or Shreveport for the Confederates; Cairo, Mound City, or St Louis for the Union. Due to the possibilities of snagging underwater obstructions such as sunken logs or debris, or of running aground on one of the countless frequently moving mud banks on the rivers, night operations were rare. When darkness fell, gunboats operating independently of major garrisons or bases would choose the safer bank, then moor alongside for the night. Armed sentries would be posted on deck and on shore and, if the area was considered dangerous, steam pressure would be maintained to permit a rapid response to any threat should it occur.

Sailors caulking the hull of a wooden gunboat. This involved the wedging of tarred hemp into the cracks between the vessel's outer planking. As most river ports lacked the facilities to raise gunboat hulls out of the water, repairs were usually confined to what could be done above the waterline. (Author's collection)

Each crew was divided into watches, usually divided into port and starboard, then first and last. This meant that, at any time, a quarter of the crew would be available to operate the ship, day or night, in port, at anchor, or moored alongside a hostile shore. If the commanding officer deemed it appropriate, the routine would be changed, so that the crew operated in two watches. Reveille (all hands) was piped at 5 a.m., followed by cleaning of the ship, then breakfast, which was served at 8 a.m. The vessel would then be ready to start her operations.

Noon marked the official start of the ship's day, and was the hour when the main meal of the day was served (usually meat, vegetables and coffee). Afternoons were usually spent at drill. Around 4 p.m., the vessel was moored for the night, and the crew were given a few hours to themselves before lights out.

When the vessel was not on active duty, the daylight hours would be spent painting the ship, maintaining the engines or guns, or cleaning. Unless the vessel was in its home port, where it could be rolled out of the water, maintenance work was limited to the hull and superstructure above the waterline. Sundays were deemed "make and mend" day, when the crew could wash or repair clothing, or engage in socialising. Shore leave was granted in friendly ports, many of which contained the traditional sources of amusement for sailors ashore found the world over. When the crew were unable to enjoy their leisure hours ashore, they spent their time fishing, playing cards, writing (for the few crewmen who were literate), or playing music. Almost every ship on either side had a pet, and these mascots were fed and tended in these leisure hours.

For the Confederates, supply of food, pay, and clothing was a constant struggle, while for their Union counterparts, supply problems were for the most part overcome by the summer of 1862. By 1863 bases such as Cairo or Mound City maintained floating warehouses, receiving ships, maintenance workshops, and administrative offices. While naval uniforms were hard to come by at first, both sides introduced regular navy blues (whites in summer) during the first year of the war, giving the vessels the appearance of regular warships. Although cramped, humid and uncomfortable, life on board these wooden gunboats was reasonably bearable, at least when the vessels were not engaged in action. Conditions in action were a different story.

A rare photograph of an unidentified Confederate seaman. When uniforms were issued to Confederate sailors on the western rivers, they were usually modelled on prewar US Navy uniforms. This sailor was less fortunate, and wears a thick homespun shirt.

Gunboats in Action

When the war began, nobody who was given command of a wooden gunboat on the Mississippi River knew what to expect when his vessel went into action. Although experienced naval officers had read the latest theoretical treatises and kept abreast of the latest developments in naval and ordnance technology, the effect of shell guns, steam engines and even armor cladding were largely untested when the war began. Similarly, the introduction of the ram was an unknown quantity. The gunboat captains on the Mississippi would have to learn their trade the hard way. An examination of three actions involving gunboats, at New Orleans (April 24, 1862), Plum Point (May 10, 1862), and Memphis (June 6, 1862), will provide a broad outline of the strengths and limitations of these little warships.

The river approach to New Orleans was protected by two forts: Fort Jackson on the western shore of the Mississippi, and Fort St Philip on the east. To augment the 128 guns in these fortified positions, the Confederates had towed down the unfinished ironclad *Louisiana* and moored her as a floating battery. The small ironclad ram CSS *Manassas* and a flotilla of 10 wooden gunboats took up positions upriver from the forts. Overall command of both shore and naval defenses was given to General Mansfield Lovell.

At 2 a.m. on April 24, Commodore Farragut's wooden steam fleet approached the forts, trying to bypass the static defenses. He broke through a line of rafts and hulks opposite Fort Jackson, only to have his fleet attacked by the *Manassas*. This ironclad rammed the USS *Mississippi* and the USS *Brooklyn*, but caused minimal damage. As Fort Jackson was bypassed, it was up to the gunners in Fort St Philip and the wooden gunboat fleet to stop the Union attack.

The leading Union ship was the USS *Varuna*, and the *Governor Moore* of the Louisiana Provisional Navy charged past the milling crowd of Confederate vessels to attack her. In the process she rammed and sank a Confederate tug which got in the way. Fire from the Union ships was intense. As the Confederate captain recalled, "This combined attack killed and wounded a large number of our men and cut the vessel up terribly. Suddenly two, then one Confederate ram(s) darted through the thick smoke from the right to the left bank of the river, passing close to all of us." These vessels ran aground or were disabled before they could ram any of the Union vessels.

The *Governor Moore* was more fortunate. Her commander (Captain Beverley Kennon, Louisiana Provisional Navy) ordered oil to be poured on his furnaces to generate more power, then aimed his ram at the *Varuna*. He opened fire on her with her bow gun, then rammed the Union warship. Unable to depress the bow gun sufficiently to hit the enemy hull in the normal way, the Confederate gun crew fired through the bow of their own vessel. The second such shot disabled the *Varuna*'s bow gun. "We backed clear, gathered headway again, and rammed her a second time as near the same place as possible." The *Varuna* drifted inshore, where her crew tried to beach her, but then the ram *Stonewall Jackson* came up and finished the job, sinking the Union gunboat in shallow water.

The wooden cottonclad ram *Stonewall Jackson* depicted ramming the damaged wooden gunboat USS *Varuna*. The Union vessel sank, but the Confederate ram was subsequently raked by the remainder of the Union fleet, then scuttled by her own crew.

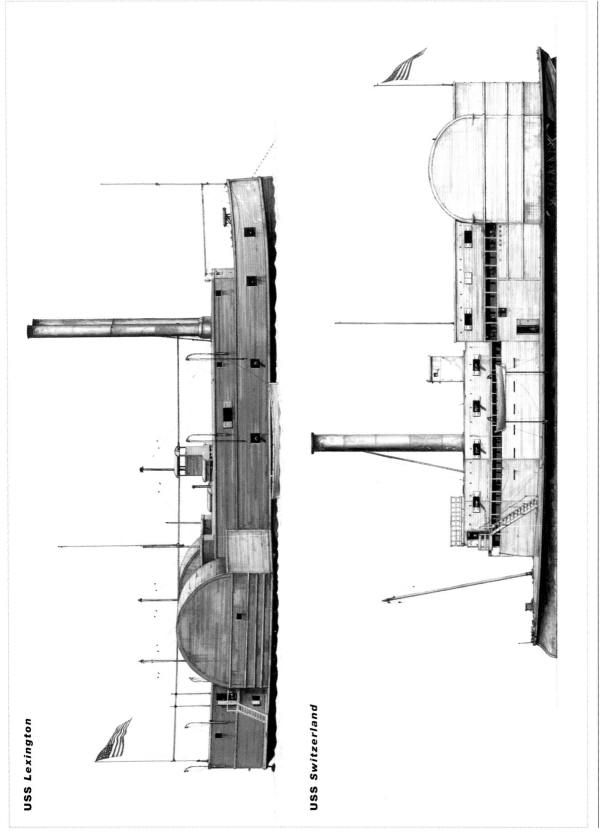

USS *Lexington*

USS *Switzerland*

A

B

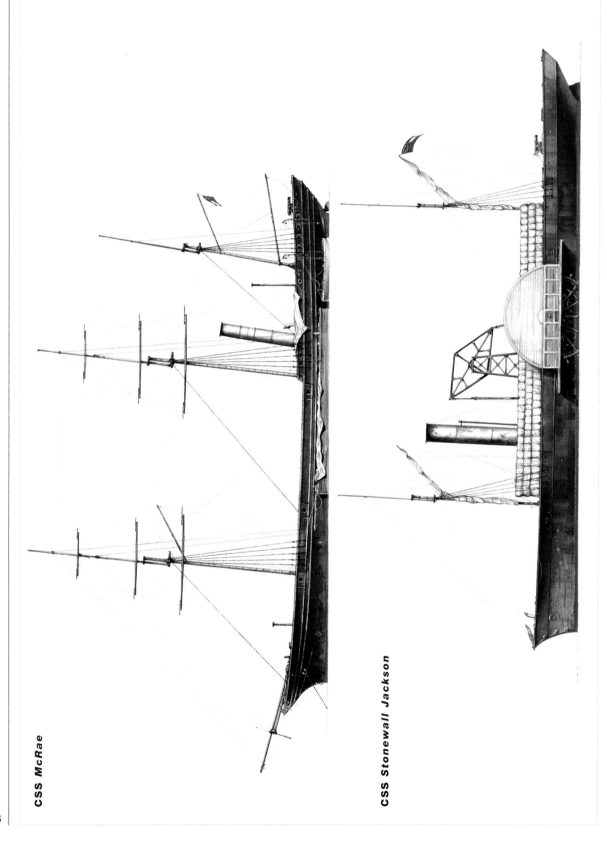

CSS *McRae*

CSS *Stonewall Jackson*

The *Governor Moore* and the USS *Varuna* at the Battle of New Orleans, April 1862

C

USS *QUEEN OF THE WEST*

D

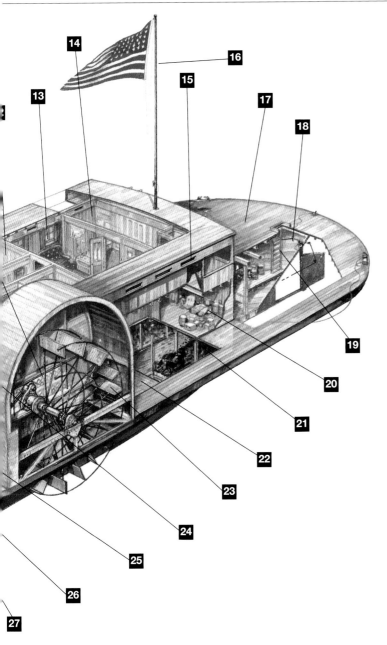

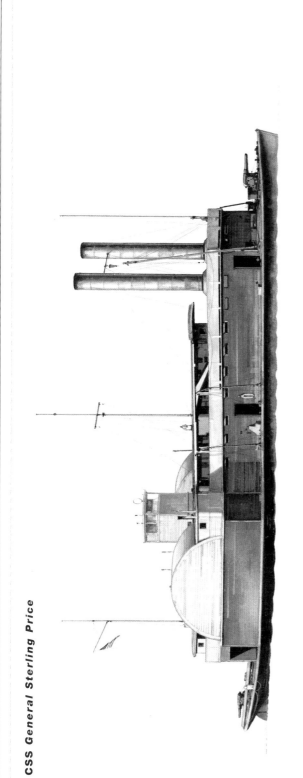

CSS *General Sterling Price*

CSS *General Bragg*

The USS *Tyler* fighting the CSS *Arkansas* on the Yazoo River, July 1862

F

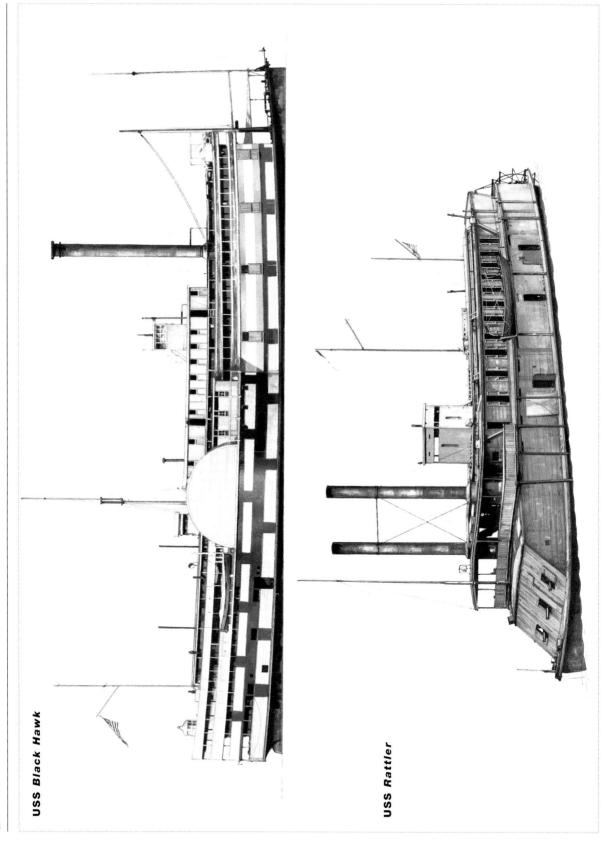

USS Black Hawk

USS Rattler

G

Minutes later the *Governor Moore* was engaged by the USS *Cayuga*, followed by the rest of the Union flotilla as they steamed past, and she was riddled with shellfire. Burning from stem to stern, she sank, her Louisiana state colors still flying. The badly damaged *Stonewall Jackson* was also abandoned.

Further downstream the CSS *McRae* also engaged the line of passing Union ships, exchanging broadsides with the powerful USS *Brooklyn* and the USS *Iroquois* before the rest of the fleet began to pour fire into her. Riddled and sinking, she was beached and abandoned by her crew. The same fate befell most of the Confederate wooden gunboats in the fleet. Unable to prevent the Union progress, they were cut off from their line of retreat up the river. The few vessels that survived the fight were destroyed by their own crews to prevent capture. Although the effectiveness of ramming tactics had been demonstrated, these gunboats had also proven their vulnerability to enemy shellfire.

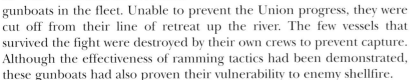

The Louisiana State cottonclad ram *Governor Moore* shown locked in combat with the gunboat USS *Varuna*, after ramming her, during the Battle of New Orleans. The Confederate gunners fired through their own hull in order to hit the enemy vessel.

On May 10, 1862, the Union river fleet was above Fort Pillow, providing cover for mortar boats which were bombarding the Confederate positions. The vessel on point guard furthest downstream was the casemate ironclad USS *Cincinnati*. Smoke was spotted, and as the ironclad raised steam, Captain James E. Montgomery's River Defense Fleet rounded the bend. Montgomery commanded his full flotilla of eight rams, and led the way in his flagship, CSS *Little Rebel*. His vessels were making approximately nine knots, steaming against a one-knot current. The Confederates had the advantage of surprise, and before the *Cincinnati* could get fully under way the CSS *General Bragg* rammed her on her starboard side. The *Cincinnati* replied with a broadside at point-blank range, sending the large wooden ram reeling downstream. Just then the CSS *General Sterling Price* smashed into the ironclad's stern, disabling her rudder.

By this time other ironclads had entered the fight, and the USS *Carondolet* and the USS *Mound City* poured fire into the *General Bragg*, which drifted away, out of the fight. The CSS *General Sumter* was the next vessel to smash into the *Cincinnati*, causing severe damage. The leading mortar boat fired mortar shells over the *Sumter* to prevent sharpshooters on her decks firing into the ironclad. The CSS *General Van Dorn* replied by firing two 32-pounder shells into the mortar boat, disabling it completely. The ram then steamed past and rammed the *Mound City*, just seconds after the ironclad was rammed by the *Sumter*. The ironclad limped off, and sank in shallow water. Next, the ironclad USS *Benton* arrived and fired on the CSS *Colonel Lovell*, while the *Carondolet* hit the *Sumter*'s boiler, which exploded, causing heavy casualties.

An aerial representation of Commodore Farragut's Union fleet forcing its way past the forts below New Orleans on April 24, 1862. In the bottom right corner, a number of Confederate gunboats are shown supporting the attack of the ironclad ram CSS *Manassas*.

Faced with annihilation, Montgomery withdrew the remainder of his force. As he now faced the entire Union river ironclad fleet, he had little option. As the *Benton* and *Carondolet* gave chase, the *Cincinnati* sank in 11 feet of water, the last casualty of the battle. In an engagement that had only lasted about 40 minutes, two Union ironclads had been sunk for the loss of 108 men, and in return for heavy damage to three Confederate rams. Once more the effectiveness of ramming tactics had been demonstrated, this time against an armored opponent. Although what became known as the Battle of Plum Point was a Confederate victory, Montgomery could ill afford such losses, and both Union ironclads were raised and repaired. Next time the two fleets met, the North would have rams of their own.

On June 6, 1862, the two fleets met again off Memphis in a dawn battle, watched by numerous onlookers on the shore. Once again, the Confederates fielded eight vessels, as the extensive damage to the ram fleet had been repaired. Five Union ironclads came downriver stern first, followed by five wooden Ellet rams (*Queen of the West, Monarch, Switzerland, Lancaster,* and *Lioness*). When the vessels came within range, the Union ironclads turned to face the enemy and the rams charged past them. The Confederate rams formed into two lines, each of four ships, and steamed to meet them. The CSS *M. Jeff Thompson* fired the first shot, and soon every ship was firing. The *Colonel Lovell* and the *General Beauregard* headed toward Ellet's flagship, the *Queen of the West*, but at the last minute the Confederate rams reversed their paddles to slow themselves down, which made them turn. Ellet smashed into the side of the *Lovell*, toppling the Confederate vessel's smokestacks and leaving her filling with water. She drifted off to the eastern shore and sank, taking most of her crew with her. The *Beauregard* duly rammed the *Queen of the West* on her port wheelhouse, and the Union vessel limped away. Ellet was mortally wounded by a sharpshooter during the clash, and he died shortly afterwards. The *Beauregard* had virtually stopped in the water by this time, and the *Monarch* headed straight for her. The *General Sumter* steered for the *Monarch*, but the Union ram slipped past the two Confederate vessels, and the *Sumter* and *Beauregard* collided. Helpless, the *Beauregard* was fired on by the ironclad *Benton*, and her boiler was hit. The Confederate ram exploded, as did the *M. Jeff Thompson*. The remaining Confederate rams turned and fled, but one by one they were disabled and destroyed by the ironclads. Only the *Earl Van Dorn* escaped to the safety of Vicksburg.

This last great ram battle on the Mississippi River not only demonstrated the vulnerability of wooden gunboats to the fire of heavy shell guns, but it virtually destroyed the last remaining Confederate naval units on the river. Although the Confederate Navy would have other successes on the rivers, its gunboat fleet had been decimated. Ramming tactics were effective, but the action also demonstrated the need to combine the ram with a powerful armament. Union leaders took this lesson to heart, and upgraded the armament of their wooden fleet.

These three river gunboat actions were characterized by close-range mêlées involving ramming and point-blank gunfire. Ramming tactics worked when the attacker had the benefit of surprise. Without it, wooden rams and gunboats simply invited destruction at the hands of more powerful warships.

After ramming the *Varuna*, the Confederate ram *Governor Moore* was devastated by fire from the Union fleet. In this engraving the USS *Pensacola* is shown pouring fire into the stricken gunboat.

SHIP LIST – UNION

Note that the entries include the vessel's principal area of operation, and where applicable, the identifying number painted on the pilot house from June 19, 1863, onwards. Where appropriate, vessels are listed by type, and in the order in which they entered service. Where no figures are given in length, displacement or other categories this means that the information was never recorded.

USS = United States Ship

NAME	TYPE	COMMISSIONED	SERVED	DISPLACEMENT
TIMBERCLADS				
USS *Tyler*	Sidewheel gunboat	June 1861	Mississippi and Tennessee Rivers	420 tons
USS *Conestoga*	Sidewheel gunboat	August 1861	Mississippi River	572 tons
USS *Lexington*	Sidewheel gunboat	August 1861	Mississipppi River	362 tons
USS *Avenger*	Sidewheel gunboat	February 1864	Mississippi River	410 tons
RAMS				
War Department (Ellet) Rams				
USS *Mingo*	Sternwheel ram	April 1862	Mississippi River	228 tons
USS *Monarch*	Sidewheel ram	April 1862	Mississippi River	406 tons
USS *Lancaster*	Sidewheel ram	May 1862	Mississippi River	375 tons
USS *Lioness*	Sternwheel ram	May 1862	Mississippi River	198 tons
USS *Queen of the West*	Sidewheel ram	May 1862	Mississippi River	406 tons
USS *Switzerland*	Sidewheel ram	May 1862	Mississippi River	519 tons
USS *Sampson*	Sternwheel ram	May 1862	Mississippi River	230 tons
Other Rams				
USS *Vindicator*	Sidewheel ram	May 1864	Mississippi and Red Rivers	750 tons
USS *Avenger*	Sidewheel ram	February 1864	Mississippi River	410 tons
TINCLADS				
USS *Brilliant* (No. 18)	Sternwheeler	August 1862	Mississippi River	227 tons
USS *General Pillow* (No. 20)	Sidewheeler	August 1862	Mississippi and Tennessee Rivers	38 tons
USS *Fairplay* (No. 17)	Sidewheeler	September 1862	Ohio and Cumberland Rivers	162 tons
USS *St Clair* (No. 19)	Sternwheeler	September 1862	Mississippi River	203 tons
USS *Marmora* (No. 2)	Sidewheeler	October 1862	Mississippi River	207 tons
USS *Signal* (No. 8)	Sternwheeler	October 1862	Mississippi and Yazoo Rivers	190 tons
USS *Black Hawk* (not numbered)	Sidewheeler	December 1862	Mississippi River (flagship)	902 tons
USS *Forest Rose* (No. 9)	Sternwheeler	December 1862	Mississippi River	260 tons
USS *Glide* (I) (not numbered)	Sternwheeler	December 1862	Mississippi River	137 tons
USS *Juliet* (No. 4)	Sternwheeler	December 1862	Mississippi River	157 tons
USS *New Era* (No. 7)	Sternwheeler	December 1862	Mississippi and White Rivers	157 tons
USS *Rattler* (No. 1)	Sternwheeler	December 1862	Mississippi River	165 tons
USS *Romeo* (No. 3)	Sternwheeler	December 1862	Mississippi and Yazoo Rivers	175 tons
USS *Silver Lake* (No. 23)	Sternwheeler	December 1862	Mississippi and Ohio Rivers	236 tons
USS *Cricket* (No. 6)	Sternwheeler	January 1863	Mississippi and Red Rivers	178 tons
USS *Springfield* (No. 22)	Sidewheeler	January 1863	Mississippi and Ohio Rivers	146 tons

The tinclad gunboat USS *Prairie Bird* (No. 11) photographed at anchor off Vicksburg, Tennessee, following the capture of the city in July 1863. She carried eight 24-pounder howitzers, and used them twice in anger, at Eunice, Mississippi, in June 1863, and at Gaine's Landing, Arkansas, in August 1864. She is typical of the dozens of tinclad sternwheelers which served in the Union river fleet.

LENGTH	ARMAMENT	REMARKS
180 ft	6 x 8 in smoothbores, 1 x 32-pdr smoothbore + 3 x 30-pdr rifles September 1862	-
-	4 x 32-pdr smoothbores	Sunk in collision, March 1864
178 ft	2 x 32-pdr smoothbores, 4 x 8 in smoothbores + 2 x 30-pdr rifles September 1862	-
210 ft	6 guns	-
-	-	Sunk in collision, November 1862
-	-	Sunk by ice damage, December 1864
176 ft	-	Sunk by Confederate gunfire at Vicksburg, March 1863
-	-	-
181 ft	4 guns	Captured by Confederates, February 1863; destroyed in action, April 1863
178 ft	-	-
-	2 guns	Converted into a floating machine shop from September 1862
210 ft	5 guns	-
210 ft	6 guns	-
155 ft	4 guns	-
81 ft	2 guns	Former Confederate steamer, captured June 1862
139 ft	4 guns	Former Confederate transport, captured August 1862
156 ft	4 guns	-
155 ft	2 x 24-pdr, 2 x 12-pdr rifles + 4 x 24-pdr	-
157 ft	7 guns	Destroyed to prevent capture, May 1864
260 ft	2 x 32-pdr, 2 x 30-pdr rifles, 2 x 12-pdr smoothbore	Burned and sunk in accidental fire, April 1865
155 ft	6 guns	-
-	6 guns	Burned and sunk in accidental fire, February 1863
156 ft	6 guns	-
137 ft	-	-
-	6 guns	Sunk in storm, December 1864
154 ft	6 guns	-
155 ft	6 guns	-
154 ft	6 guns	-
140 ft	6 guns	-

NAME	TYPE	COMMISSIONED	SERVED	DISPLACEMENT
TINCLADS (CONTINUED)				
USS *Linden* (No. 10)	Sternwheeler	January 1863	Mississippi and Arkansas Rivers	177 tons
USS *Prairie Bird* (No. 11)	Sternwheeler	January 1863	Mississippi and Yazoo Rivers	171 tons
USS *Curlew* (No. 12)	Sternwheeler	February 1863	Mississippi River	196 tons
USS *Covington* (No. 25)	Sidewheeler	February 1863	Tennessee River	224 tons
USS *Petrel* (No. 5)	Sternwheeler	February 1863	Mississippi River	226 tons
USS *Argosy* (No. 27)	Sternwheeler	March 1863	Mississippi River	219 tons
USS *Hastings* (No. 15)	Sidewheeler	April 1863	Tennessee and White Rivers	196 tons
USS *Queen City* (No. 26)	Sidewheeler	April 1863	Mississippi and Tennessee Rivers	210 tons
USS *Champion* (No. 24)	Sternwheeler	April 1863	Mississippi River	115 tons
USS *James Thompson* (No. 13)	Sidewheeler	April 1863	Mississippi and Red Rivers	280 tons
USS *Naumkeag* (No. 37)	Sternwheeler	April 1863	Mississippi River	148 tons
USS *Fawn* (No. 30)	Sternwheeler	May 1863	White River	174 tons
USS *Kenwood* (No. 14)	Sternwheeler	May 1863	Mississippi and Arkansas Rivers	232 tons
USS *Key West* (No. 32)	Sternwheeler	May 1863	Mississippi and Tennessee Rivers	207 tons
USS *Moose* (No. 34)	Sternwheeler	May 1863	Mississippi River	189 tons
USS *Silver Cloud* (No. 28)	Sternwheeler	May 1863	Mississippi River	236 tons
USS *Alfred Robb* (No. 21)	Sternwheeler	May 1863	Mississippi River	86 tons
USS *Exchange* (No. 38)	Sternwheeler	June 1863	Tennessee and Yazoo Rivers	211 tons
USS *Reindeer* (No. 35)	Sternwheeler	July 1863	Mississippi River	212 tons
USS *Victory* (No. 33)	Sidewheeler	July 1863	Mississippi and Ohio Rivers	160 tons
USS *Paw Paw* (No. 31)	Centerwheeler	July 1863	Mississippi River	175 tons
USS *Peosta* (No. 36)	Sidewheeler	October 1863	Mississippi and Tennessee Rivers	204 tons
USS *Tawah* (No. 29)	Sidewheeler	October 1863	Mississippi and Tennessee Rivers	108 tons
USS *Glide* (II) (No. 43)	Sternwheeler	November 1863	Gulf of Mexico	232 tons
USS *Wave* (No. 45)	Sternwheeler	November 1863	Gulf of Mexico	229 tons
USS *Stockdale* (No. 42)	Sternwheeler	December 1863	Gulf of Mexico	188 tons
USS *Alexandria* (No. 40)	Sidewheeler	December 1863	Mississippi River	60 tons
USS *Nyanza* (No. 41)	Sidewheeler	December 1863	Mississippi River	203 tons
USS *Ouachita* (not numbered)	Sidewheeler	January 1864	Mississippi River	572 tons
USS *Tensas* (No. 39)	Sidewheeler	February 1864	Mississippi River	62 tons
USS *Gazelle* (No. 50)	Sidewheeler	February 1864	Red River	117 tons
USS *Elfin* (No. 52)	Sternwheeler	February 1864	Mississippi River	192 tons
USS *Fairy* (No. 51)	Sternwheeler	March 1864	Mississippi River	173 tons
USS *Meteor* (No. 44)	Sternwheeler	March 1864	Gulf of Mexico	221 tons
USS *Naiad* (No. 53)	Sternwheeler	April 1864	Mississippi River	185 tons
USS *Nymph* (No. 54)	Sternwheeler	April 1864	Mississippi River	171 tons

The former luxury river steam boat *New Uncle Sam* was commissioned as the USS *Black Hawk*, and served as a floating command vessel for Admiral Porter during the siege of Vicksburg and the Red River campaign.

LENGTH	ARMAMENT	REMARKS
154 ft	6 guns	Sunk after striking object in water, February 1864
160 ft	8 guns	-
159 ft	7 guns	-
126 ft	8 guns	Abandoned and destroyed, May 1864
-	8 guns	Captured by Confederates, then destroyed, April 1864
156 ft	8 guns	-
164 ft	7 guns	-
-	8 guns	Captured by Confederates, then destroyed, June 1864
146 ft	5 guns	
150 ft	6 guns	Renamed *Manitou* in June 1863, and *Fort Hindman* in November 1863
154 ft	6 guns	-
159 ft	6 guns	-
154 ft	5 guns	-
156 ft	6 guns	Destroyed to prevent capture, November 1864
155 ft	10 guns	-
155 ft	6 guns	-
115 ft	4 guns	Former Confederate transport, captured in April 1862
155 ft	6 guns	-
154 ft	6 guns	-
157 ft	6 guns	-
120 ft	8 guns	Sunk after striking underwater obstacle, August 1863; salvaged and repaired, September 1863
151 ft	14 guns	-
114 ft	8 guns	Destroyed to prevent capture, November 1864
160 ft	6 guns	-
154 ft	6 guns	Captured by Confederates, May 1864
-	6 guns	-
90 ft	2 guns	Confederate gunboat, captured in July 1863
-	6 guns	-
227 ft	5 x 30-pdr rifles, 18 x 24-pdr, 15 x 12-pdr, smoothbores, 1 x 12-pdr	Former Confederate riverboat
92 ft	2 guns	Former Confederate gunboat
135 ft	6 guns	-
155 ft	8 guns	Burned to prevent capture, November 1864
157 ft	8 guns	-
156 ft	6 guns	-
157 ft	12 guns	-
161 ft	12 guns	-

The tinclad USS *Peosta* (No. 36) was converted from a Cincinnati riverboat bearing the same name in late 1863. She operated on the Mississippi and Tennessee Rivers, and used her powerful armament of 14 guns (including three 30-pounder rifles) to bombard enemy troop concentrations at Paducah, Kentucky, in March 1864. (Mariners' Museum)

NAME	TYPE	COMMISSIONED	SERVED	DISPLACEMENT
TINCLADS (CONTINUED)				
USS *Tallahatchie* (No. 46)	Sternwheeler	April 1864	Mississippi River	171 tons
USS *Undine* (No. 55)	Sternwheeler	April 1864	Mississippi River	179 tons
USS *Carrabasset* (No. 49)	Sidewheeler	May 1864	Gulf of Mexico	202 tons
USS *Elk* (No. 47)	Sidewheeler	May 1864	Gulf of Mexico	162 tons
USS *Rodolph* (No. 48)	Sternwheeler	May 1864	Gulf of Mexico	217 tons
USS *Huntress* (No. 58)	Sternwheeler	June 1864	Mississippi River	211 tons
USS *Peri* (No. 57	Sternwheeler	June 1864	Mississippi River	155 tons
USS *Sibyl* (No. 59)	Sternwheeler	June 1864	Mississippi River	176 tons
USS *General Sherman* (No. 60)	Sidewheeler	July 1864	Tennessee River	187 tons
USS *General Grant* (No. 62)	Sidewheeler	July 1864	Tennessee River	204 tons
USS *General Thomas* (No. 61)	Sidewheeler	August 1864	Tennessee River	184 tons
USS *General Burnside* (No. 63)	Sidewheeler	August 1864	Tennessee River (flagship)	210 tons
USS *Siren* (No. 56)	Sternwheeler	August 1864	Receiving Ship, Mississippi River	232 tons
USS *Grossbeak* (No. 8)	Sidewheeler	February 1865	Mississippi River	196 tons
USS *Colossus* (No. 25)	Sternwheeler	February 1865	Mississippi River	183 tons
USS *Mist* (No. 26)	Sternwheeler	March 1865	Mississippi River	232 tons
USS *Oriole* (No. 52)	Sternwheeler	March 1865	Mississippi River	236 tons
USS *Gamage* (No. 60)	Sternwheeler	March 1865	Mississippi River	187 tons
USS *Collier* (No. 29)	Sternwheeler	March 1865	Mississippi River	176 tons
USS *Ibex* (No. 10)	Sidewheeler	April 1865	Mississippi River	235 tons
USS *Kate* (No. 55)	Sternwheeler	April 1865	Mississippi River	241 tons
USS *Tempest* (No. 1)	Sternwheeler	April 1865	Mississippi River (flagship)	161 tons
USS *Abeona* (No. 32)	Sidewheeler	April 1865	Mississippi River	206 tons
CAPTURED VESSELS NOT PREVIOUSLY LISTED				
USS *General Bragg*	-	-	Mississippi and Yazoo Rivers	-
USS *General Price*	-	-	Mississippi and Red Rivers	-
USS *Sumter*	-	-	Mississippi River and Gulf of Mexico	-
USS *Barataria*	-	-	Gulf of Mexico	-
USS *Little Rebel* (16)	-	-	Mississippi River	-

The tinclad USS *Naiad* (No. 53) entered service in the spring of 1864 and saw action during a series of engagements with Confederate shore batteries in Louisiana. Before being bought by the US Navy, she was the *Princess*, a passenger steamer operating on the Ohio River.

LENGTH	ARMAMENT	REMARKS
-	6 guns	-
-	8 guns	Captured by Confederates, October 1864; burned to prevent recapture, November 1864
155 ft	6 guns	-
156 ft	6 guns	-
	6 guns	Sunk by mine, April 1865
132 ft	6 guns	-
148 ft	7 guns	-
150 ft	4 guns	-
168 ft	5 guns	Decommissioned by Navy, March 1865
171 ft	5 guns	-
165 ft	5 guns	-
171 ft	5 guns	-
155 ft	8 guns	-
164 ft	7 guns	-
115 ft	7 guns	-
157 ft	7 guns	-
125 ft	9 guns	-
148 ft	9 guns	-
158 ft	9 guns	-
157 ft	7 guns	-
160 ft	10 guns	-
162 ft	8 guns	-
157 ft	5 guns	-
-	-	Formerly the CSS *General Bragg*; details listed in Confederate entry
-	-	Formerly the CSS *General Sterling Price*; details listed in Confederate entry
-	-	Formerly the CSS *General Sumter*; details listed in Confederate entry; ran aground and abandoned, August 1862
-	-	Formerly the CSS *Barataria*; details listed in Confederate entry; burned to prevent capture, April 1863
-	-	Formally CSS *Little Rebel*; details listed in Confederate entry

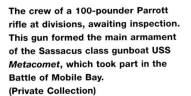

The crew of a 100-pounder Parrott rifle at divisions, awaiting inspection. This gun formed the main armament of the Sassacus class gunboat USS *Metacomet*, which took part in the Battle of Mobile Bay. (Private Collection)

SHIP LIST – CONFEDERATE

CSS = Confederate States Ship; LSNS = Louisiana State Navy Ship

NAME	TYPE	COMMISSIONED	SERVED	DISPLACEMENT
THE NEW ORLEANS SQUADRON				
CSS *McRae*	Screw gunboat	March 1861	-	680 tons
CSS *Jackson*	Sidewheel gunboat	May 1861	-	297 tons
LSNS *General Quitman*	Sidewheel cottonclad ram	February 1862	-	945 tons
LSNS *Governor Moore*	Sidewheel cottonclad ram	January 1862	-	1,215 tons
CSS *Warrior*	Sidewheel cottonclad ram	March 1862	-	-
CSS *Stonewall Jackson*	Sidewheel cottonclad gunboat	March 1862	-	-
CSS *Defiance*	Sidewheel gunboat	December 1861	-	544 tons
CSS *Resolute*	Sidewheel gunboat	March 1862	-	-
CSS *General Lovell*	Sidewheel ram	March 1862	-	-
CSS *General Breckenridge*	Sternwheel gunboat	April 1862	-	-
OTHER VESSELS AT NEW ORLEANS				
CSS *Anglo-Saxon*	Sidewheel gunboat	January 1862	-	508 tons
CSS *Arrow*	Screw gunboat	March 1862	-	-
CSS *Mosher*	Screw tugboat	-	-	-
CSS *Star*	Screw tugboat	-	-	-
CSS *Phoenix*	Screw tugboat	-	-	-
CSS *Landis*	Sidewheel tender	-	-	-
CSS *W. Burton*	Sidewheel tender	-	-	-
THE RIVER DEFENSE FLEET				
CSS *Little Rebel*	Sidewheel cottonclad ram	February 1862	-	161 tons
CSS *General Bragg*	Sidewheel cottonclad gunboat	March 1862	-	1,024 tons
CSS *General Sterling Price*	Sidewheel cottonclad ram	January 1862	-	633 tons
CSS *General Sumter*	Sidewheel cottonclad ram	February 1862	-	524 tons
CSS *General Earl Van Dorn*	Sidewheel cottonclad ram	April 1862	-	-
CSS *General M. Jeff Thompson*	Sidewheel cottonclad ram	April 1862	-	-
CSS *Colonel Lovell*	Sidewheel cottonclad ram	November 1861	-	521 tons
CSS *General Beauregard*	Sidewheel cottonclad ram	April 1862	-	454 tons
OTHER CONFEDERATE GUNBOATS OPERATING ON THE MISSISSIPPI				
CSS *Calhoun*	Sidewheel gunboat	June 1861	-	508 tons
CSS *Ivy*	Sidewheel gunboat	as privateer in May 1861	-	447 tons
CSS *James L. Day*	Sidewheel gunboat	May 1861	-	414 tons
CSS *Oregon*	Sidewheel gunboat	June 1861	-	532 tons

LENGTH	ARMAMENT	REMARKS
-	8 guns	Sunk following heavy damage in action, April 1862
-	2 guns	Destroyed to prevent capture, April 1862
230 ft	2 guns	Destroyed to prevent capture, April 1862
220 ft	2 guns	Destroyed in action, April 1862
-	1 gun	Destroyed in action, April 1862
-	1 gun	Destroyed in action, April 1862
178 ft	1 gun	Destroyed to prevent capture, April 1862
-	2 guns	Destroyed to prevent capture, April 1862
-	1 gun	Destroyed to prevent capture, April 1862
-	1 gun	Destroyed to prevent capture, April 1862
120 ft	-	Damaged and abandoned, April 1862; salvaged, and used as a Union transport
-	1 gun	Destroyed to prevent capture, June 1862
-	-	Sunk in action, April 1862
-	-	Sunk in action, April 1862
-	-	Sunk in action, April 1862
-	-	Damaged in action and captured, April 1862
-	-	Damaged in action and captured, April 1862
-	3 guns	Ran aground and captured, June 1862; later used in Union service
208 ft	2 guns	Ran aground and captured, June 1862; later used in Union service
182 ft	4 guns	Sunk in action, June 1862; later salvaged and used in Union service
182 ft	5 guns	Ran aground and captured, June 1862; later used in Union service
	1 gun	Burned to prevent capture, June 1862
	-	Sunk in action, June 1862
162 ft	4 guns	Sunk in action, June 1862
162 ft	5 guns	Sunk at action, June 1862
174 ft	3 guns	Captured, January 1862, and later used in Union service; transferred to US Army, June 1864, and renamed *General Sedgewick*
191 ft	4 guns	Destroyed to prevent capture, May 1863
187 ft	-	Fate unknown, but probably destroyed to prevent capture, April 1862
217 ft	4 guns	Destroyed to prevent capture, April 1862

NAME	TYPE	COMMISSIONED	SERVED	DISPLACEMENT
OTHER CONFEDERATE GUNBOATS OPERATING ON THE MISSISSIPPI (CONTINUED)				
CSS *Barataria*	Sternwheel ironclad gunboat	September 1861	-	400 tons
CSS *Tuscarora*	Sidewheel gunboat	August 1861	Mississippi and Arkansas Rivers	-
CSS *Webb*	Sidewheel cottonclad ram	January 1862	Mississippi and Red Rivers	655 tons
CSS *Pamlico*	Sidewheel gunboat	September 1861	Lake Pontchartrain	218 tons
CSS *General Polk*	Sidewheel gunboat	October 1861	Mississippi and Yazoo Rivers	390 tons
CSS *Grand Duke*	Sidewheel cottonclad gunboat	February 1863	Red River	508 tons
CSS *J.A. Cotton*	Sidewheel cottonclad gunboat	March 1863	Red River	372 tons
CSS *Livingston*	Sidewheel gunboat	February 1862	Mississippi and Yazoo Rivers	-
CSS *Maurepas*	Sidewheel gunboat	November 1861	Mississippi and White Rivers	399 tons
CSS *Pontchartrain*	Sidewheel gunboat	March 1862	Mississippi and Red Rivers	454 tons
CSS *St Mary*	Sidewheel gunboat	September 1862	Yazoo River	60 tons
CSS *Tom Sugg*	Sidewheel gunboat	August 1861	White River	62 tons

FURTHER READING

Bauer, Jack K., and Roberts, Stephen S.; *Register of Ships of the US Navy, 1775-1990*, Greenwood Press (Westport, CT, 1991)

Bennett, Frank M.; *The Steam Navy of the United States*, Warren and Company (Pittsburgh, PA, 1896)

Canney, Donald L.; *Lincoln's Navy; The Ships, Men and Organization, 1861–65*, Conway Maritime Press (London, UK, 1998)

Coombe, Jack D.; *Thunder along the Mississippi: The River Battles that split the Confederacy*, Sarpedon (New York, 1996)

Jones, Virgil Carrington; *The Civil War at Sea* [2 volumes], Rinehart and Winston (New York, 1960), reprinted in 3 volumes by Broadfoot Press (Wilmington, NC, 1990)

Musicant, Ivan; *Divided Waters: The Naval History of the Civil War*, Castle Books (Edison, NJ, 2000)

Luraghi, Raimondo; *A History of the Confederate Navy*, Naval Institute Press (Annapolis, MD, 1996)

Silverstone, Paul H.; *Warships of the Civil War Navies*, Naval Institute Press (Annapolis, MD, 1989)

Still, William N., (ed.); *The Confederate Navy; The Ships, Men and Organization, 1861–65*, Naval Institute Press and Conway Maritime Press (Annapolis, MD, and London, UK, 1997)

Underwood, Robert, and Buel, Clarence Clough, (eds.) *Battles and Leaders of the Civil War* [Four Volumes], Century Company (New York, 1887), reprinted by Castle (Edison, NJ, 1987). Note that this source contains articles originally published in *Century Magazine*, including accounts by participants in the river battles on the Mississippi.

Official Records of the Union and Confederate Navies in the War of the Rebellion [30 volumes], Government Printing Office (Washington, DC, 1894–1921)

COLOR PLATE COMMENTARY

PLATE A
USS *Lexington*

One of the first three Union gunboats to see service on the Mississippi River, the 362-ton USS *Lexington* carried a powerful broadside armament of four 8-inch smoothbore guns, and two 32-pounders (the latter guns carried in her deckhouse). She first saw action in a skirmish with the Confederate gunboat *Jackson* off Hickman, Kentucky, in October 1861, and also participated in the capture of Fort Henry on the Tennessee River. After the fort's capture she roamed down the river as far as Florence, Alabama, during February 1862, before providing gunfire support for the army at the Battle of Shiloh in April 1862. She spearheaded other drives up the White River in Arkansas and the Yazoo River in Mississippi during 1862 before participating in the capture of Fort Hindman on the Arkansas River in January 1863. Further operations up the Mississippi tributaries in Arkansas, Louisiana, and Tennessee followed. One of the most active Union gunboats on the Mississippi, the *Lexington* survived the war, and was sold out of service in August 1865.

USS *Switzerland*

One of the rams designed by Colonel Ellet (also known as War Department Rams), the *Switzerland* entered service in May 1862, just in time to participate in the Battle of Memphis on June 6. Although she was unable to ram anything during the battle, the Ellet Ram fleet distinguished themselves, and confounded their critics. Unlike the other rams in the fleet, her tall slab sides and sharp-angled superstructure permitted the fitting of additional armament, and extra ordnance was accordingly placed in a casemate on her upper deck. She took part in a reconnaissance up the Yazoo River in Mississippi before joining the main fleet outside Vicksburg. She was damaged in March 1863 as she and the ram USS

LENGTH	ARMAMENT	REMARKS
125 ft	3 guns	Captured, April 1862; later used in Union service
	2 guns	Destroyed by accidental fire, November 1861
206 ft	3 guns	Destroyed to prevent capture, April 1865
-	4 guns	Destroyed to prevent capture, April 1862
280 ft	3 guns	Destroyed to prevent capture, June 1862
205 ft	-	Destroyed by accidental fire, September 1863
185 ft	4 guns	Surrendered to Union forces, May 1865
180 ft	6 guns	Destroyed to prevent capture, June 1862
180 ft	7 guns	Sunk as blockship, June 1862
204 ft	7 guns	Destroyed to prevent capture, October 1863
90 ft	2 guns	Captured, July 1863; later used in Union Service (as USS *Alexandria*)
92 ft	2 guns	Captured, July 1863; later used in Union service (as USS *Tensas*)

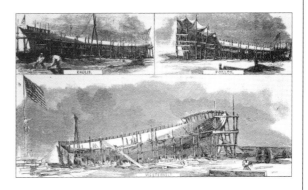

Although numerous Union ocean-going gunboats were used to enforce the naval blockade of the Confederacy, several "90-day" gunboats served on the Mississippi during 1862. These illustrations show the lack of sophisticated shipbuilding facilities needed to produce gunboats during the war. Gunboats could be and were built in primitive riverside shipyards. (Private Collection)

Lancaster ran south past the city's defenses, to link up with the ocean-going fleet below the city. Her consort was sunk. She was patched up, and repeated the action at Grand Gulf, Mississippi. For the remainder of the war she operated on the lower Mississippi and the Red River.

PLATE B
CSS *McRae*
This beautiful Confederate screw gunboat began her career in the Mexican Navy as the *Marqués de la Habana*. Her crew rebelled, and after committing acts of piracy, they were captured by the USS *Saratoga* in 1860. She was still impounded in New Orleans when Louisiana seceded, and the Confederate Navy duly purchased her. She became the backbone of the official naval presence on the lower Mississippi River. During 1861 she escorted blockade-runners out through the Mississippi Delta, then when the Union fleet established a close blockade, she attacked them in concert with other Confederate gunboats in October. Her final action took place on April 24, 1862, when the Union fleet under Commodore Farragut attacked the naval and shore defenses below New Orleans. She engaged several enemy warships at the same time, but was badly damaged. Left to founder, she limped upriver to New Orleans behind the Union fleet, then sank alongside the city wharf. She carried one 9-inch smoothbore mounted on a 180-degree pivot behind her mainmast, and a broadside armament of six 32-pounder guns, plus a small 6-pounder rifle as a bow-chaser.

CSS *Stonewall Jackson*
One of a handful of wooden vessels that had been converted into warships, the *Stonewall Jackson* had her bow reinforced with wood and iron, creating a crude ram. Armed with a single 32-pounder smoothbore gun on her quarterdeck, the small sidewheel steamer had her engine rooms, boilers and superstructure reinforced by a bulwark of cotton bales, which extended from her holds up to above her upper deck, creating a protected bridge. In the battle of New Orleans she rammed and sank the USS *Varuna*, which had already been damaged by the *Governor Moore*, but then succumbed to the combined firepower of the Union fleet as it steamed past her. She was run aground in a sinking condition on the north bank of the river near New Orleans, and was then set on fire by her crew to prevent her capture.

PLATE C
The *Governor Moore* and the USS *Varuna* at the Battle of New Orleans, April 1862
In order to control the Mississippi River, the Union needed to control New Orleans. Its southern approaches were defended by the twin forts of Fort Jackson and Fort St Philip, and by a diverse collection of rams, gunboats, tugs, and

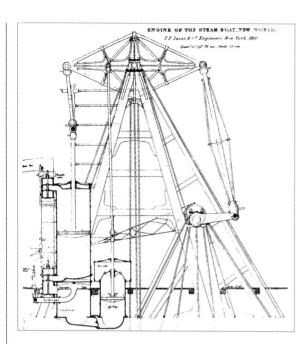

The "walking beam engine" was the most common form of engine used on the paddleboats that plied the western rivers in peace and in war. Usually the structure extended several feet above the upper deck. This is an illustration from a treatise on steam engines, dated 1852. (Private Collection)

ironclads. Before dawn on April 24, 1862, Commodore David G. Farragut led his ocean-going fleet against these defenses. Advancing in three divisions, the two leading groups were held up breaking through the line of obstructions in front of Fort Jackson, and the USS *Brooklyn* collided with the gunboat USS *Kineo*. In the confusion the Confederate ironclad ram CSS *Manassas* attacked the leading Union ships, creating more confusion. The wooden gunboat USS *Varuna* was now in the lead, followed at a distance by the rest of the fleet. The fleet of Confederate wooden rams launched an attack, but most were unable to close with the more powerful enemy warships. One exception was the *Governor Moore*, a wooden cottonclad ram in the service of the State of Louisiana. She shadowed the *Varuna*, and as the Union gunboat reached and passed the Quarantine Station, halfway between the forts and the city, the *Governor Moore* struck. She cut between the *Varuna* and the bank, then turned and rammed her amidships on her starboard side. As the two vessels were locked together, Captain Kennon of the *Governor Moore* found his bow gun was unable to fire on the enemy as the angle of fire was blocked by his own forecastle. He ordered the 32-pounder smoothbore to be fired down through his own deck, with the shot emerging through the bows of his gunboat to strike the *Varuna*. The first shot was deflected by the *Governor Moore*'s hawsepipe, but the second hit her bow gun. Next, the *Governor Moore* backed away, then as the *Varuna* turned, she rammed her again, this time on her port beam. The *Varuna* was a wreck, and a blow from the ram *Stonewall Jackson* finished her off. By this time the rest of the Union fleet had come up to the battle scene, and the *Governor Moore* was ripped apart by shellfire. She

sank with her Louisiana colors still flying. The plate depicts the scene when the *Governor Moore* fired her second shot.

PLATE D
USS *Queen of the West*
The USS *Queen of the West* was purchased by the US War Department in Cincinnati, Ohio, in May 1862, and converted into a ram, under the guidance of Colonel Charles Ellet. She served as Ellet's flagship at the Battle of Memphis in June 1862, when she rammed the Confederate wooden ram *Colonel Lovell*. Rammed in her turn by the CSS *General Sumter*, she came under fire from Confederate sharpshooters, who mortally wounded Ellet. Following repairs, she participated in the expedition up the Yazoo River which led to a running battle with the Confederate ironclad CSS *Arkansas*. She survived, and took part in operations around Vicksburg and on the Yazoo River before joining a reconnaissance expedition up the Red River into Louisiana. She ran aground in front of a Confederate fortification called Fort de Russy, on February 14, 1863, and was abandoned. The Confederates duly captured her, and she served against her former masters, participating in the sinking of the powerful ironclad USS *Indianola* near New Carthage, Mississippi, on February 24. Three weeks later, during an engagement on the Atchafalaya River in Louisiana, she was hit by a shell from the USS *Calhoun*, a former Confederate gunboat. She caught fire, and her crew abandoned ship minutes before the wooden ram exploded.

PLATE E
CSS *General Sterling Price*
One of the Confederate River Defense Fleet, the CSS *General Sterling Price* was formerly the *Laurent Millaudon*, a Cincinnati river steamer. She was acquired and converted in New Orleans, becoming a "cottonclad" ram. This conversion involved the reinforcement of the bow with a wood and iron beam, the protection of the inside of her upperworks with a compressed "sandwich" of cotton and a wooden partition, and the addition of four 9-inch smoothbores. She fought at Fort Pillow and Memphis, Tennessee, and sank within sight of the city. She was duly raised by a Union salvage team, and she entered service as a Union river gunboat. Renamed the USS *General Price*, she operated around Vicksburg until the fall of the city in July 1863, apart from a brief foray up the Red River. Subsequently she took part in the attack on Grand Gulf, Mississippi, and the Red River Expedition in 1864.

CSS *General Bragg*
The largest vessel in the Confederate River Defense Fleet, the CSS *General Bragg* began her life as a ocean-going steamship before her conversion into a warship in early 1862. Like the *General Sumter*, her bulkheads were reinforced with compressed cotton, and her bows were fitted with a crude ram. Her principal weapon was a 30-pounder Parrott rifle, a rare gun in the Confederacy, although she also carried a 32-pounder smoothbore. She took part in the river battle of Plum Point (Fort Pillow) when she rammed the ironclad USS *Cincinnati*, causing her to sink, but the Confederate gunboat was badly damaged in the process. She was repaired in time to take part in the calamitous Battle of Memphis in June 1862, when she was beached on a sandbar in a sinking condition. The *General Bragg* was raised and entered service

as a Union gunboat, patrolling the upper Mississippi for most of the remainder of the war.

PLATE F
The USS *Tyler* fighting the CSS *Arkansas* on the Yazoo River, July 1862

Like the *Lexington* and the *Conestoga*, the USS *Tyler* was one of the first Union gunboats to see service on the Mississippi River. Although small, she carried a powerful broadside armament of six 8-inch smoothbores, as well as a 32-pounder deck gun. By September 1862 she was rearmed with an additional three 30-pounder Parrott rifles. She participated in the capture of Fort Henry and Fort Donelson, then supported General Grant's army at the Battle of Shiloh. By mid-1862 the Union River fleet and the ocean-going fleet had joined forces above Vicksburg, but rumors that the Confederates were building an ironclad on the Yazoo River caused some concern. The USS *Tyler* was duly sent to investigate, accompanied by the USS *Queen of the West* and the casemate ironclad USS *Carondelet*. Soon after dawn on July 15, the three Union vessels had steamed several miles up the river when they spotted smoke coming from around a bend. The *Tyler* was well ahead of her consorts, and was the first to identify the oncoming vessel as the Confederate ironclad CSS *Arkansas*. Lieutenant William Gwin commanding the *Tyler* fired his guns, then spun around, heading back downstream. Soon the three Union vessels were fighting a running battle, and sharpshooters on the *Tyler* wounded the *Arkansas*' commander, Lieutenant Brown. Damage to the *Carondelet* forced the Union ironclad into the bank, and Brown closed and raked her, then brought his ironclad alongside and poured fire into the Union vessel at point blank range. Leaving her in a near-sinking condition, the *Arkansas* then backed away, intent on finishing off the two wooden gunboats. The *Queen of the West* fled downriver toward the safety of the Union fleet. Lieutenant Gwin wanted to fight, but left alone, he had little choice but to flee himself. Pursued by the *Arkansas*, the *Tyler* kept 200 yards ahead, and hit the Confederate ironclad in her smokestack, reducing her speed and allowing the gunboat to speed to safety. The *Arkansas* went on to run through the Union fleet to reach the safety of Vicksburg. The plate depicts the moment when

Admiral David D. Porter commanded the Union river fleets on the Mississippi and her tributaries from his command ship, the USS *Black Hawk*. Although she was not really a warship, she did carry two 30-pounder rifles and two 32-pounder smoothbores for her own protection.

The USS *Tyler* photographed at anchor during a "make and mend" Sunday, when the crew were allowed to wash or repair their uniforms. The powerful little gunboat was damaged during her engagement with the ironclad CSS *Arkansas* on the Yazoo River in July 1862.

the *Arkansas* began backing away from the wounded *Carondelet*, and the *Tyler* in the foreground was left alone to fight the victorious Confederate ironclad.

PLATE G
USS *Black Hawk*

One of the strongest gunboats on the Mississippi River, the USS *Black Hawk* was built in New Albany, Indiana, in 1848 as the luxury river steamer *New Uncle Sam*. In November 1862 she was purchased in Cairo, Illinois, for $36,000, and converted into a naval headquarters vessel for Admiral David D. Porter, the commander of the Union river forces on the Mississippi. She entered service in December 1862 when she joined the fleet above Vicksburg, and even though she was considered a tinclad warship, she still retained much of her former opulence. Palatial staircases, comfortable lounges and richly fitted state rooms gave the interior of the vessel the air of a luxury hotel, and Porter strictly enforced dress regulations and naval discipline. She also had teeth, carrying a bow armament of two 30-pounder Parrott rifles, as well as smoothbore guns. The floating headquarters was present at the capture of Fort Hindman on the Arkansas River in January 1863, the siege of Vicksburg during the summer of 1863, and the disastrous Red River campaign of 1864. She was destroyed by an accidental fire days after the end of the war, in April 1865.

USS *Rattler*

Formerly the Cincinnati-built river steamer *Florence Miller*, the USS *Rattler* was acquired by the US Navy in November 1862, and entered service five weeks later. She is included as a typical example of one of the small tinclad gunboats that served on the Mississippi and her tributaries from 1862 until the end of the war. A total of 71 such vessels served in the Union fleet during the war, most of them seeing extensive service. Powered by a stern paddlewheel, the *Rattler* was armed with two bow-mounted 30-pounder Parrott rifles and a 24-pounder smoothbore, while another three guns were carried inside her tinclad hull casemate on pivot mounts. The *Rattler* took part in the capture of Fort Hindman on the Arkansas River, then operated extensively in the river networks of Louisiana before she collided with an underwater obstruction and was wrecked near Grand Gulf, Mississippi, in December 1864.

INDEX

Figures in **bold** refer to illustrations

COMPANION SERIES FROM OSPREY

ESSENTIAL HISTORIES
Concise studies of the motives, methods and repercussions of human conflict, spanning history from ancient times to the present day. Each volume studies one major war or arena of war, providing an indispensable guide to the fighting itself, the people involved, and its lasting impact on the world around it.

MEN-AT-ARMS
The uniforms, equipment, insignia, history and organization of the world's military forces from earliest times to the present day. Authoritative text and full-color artwork, photographs and diagrams bring over 5000 years of history vividly to life.

ELITE
This series focuses on uniforms, equipment, insignia and unit histories in the same way as Men-at-Arms but in more extended treatments of larger subjects, also including personalities and techniques of warfare.

CAMPAIGN
Accounts of history's greatest conflicts, detailing the command strategies, tactics, movements and actions of the opposing forces throughout the crucial stages of each campaign. Full-color battle scenes, 3-dimensional 'bird's-eye views', photographs and battle maps guide the reader through each engagement from its origins to its conclusion.

ORDER OF BATTLE
The greatest battles in history, featuring unit-by-unit examinations of the troops and their movements as well as analysis of the commanders' original objectives and actual achievements. Color maps including a large fold-out base map, organizational diagrams and photographs help the reader to trace the course of the fighting in unprecedented detail.

WARRIOR
Insights into the daily lives of history's fighting men and women, past and present, detailing their motivation, training, tactics, weaponry and experiences. Meticulously researched narrative and full-color artwork, photographs, and scenes of battle and daily life provide detailed accounts of the experiences of combatants through the ages.

AIRCRAFT OF THE ACES
Portraits of the elite pilots of the 20th century's major air campaigns, including unique interviews with surviving aces. Unit listings, scale plans and full-color artwork combine with the best archival photography available to provide a detailed insight into the experience of war in the air.

COMBAT AIRCRAFT
The world's greatest military aircraft and combat units and their crews, examined in detail. Each exploration of the leading technology, men and machines of aviation history is supported by unit listings and other data, artwork, scale plans, and archival photography.

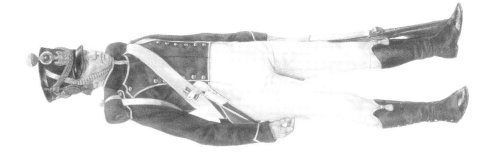 

OSPREY
PUBLISHING

FIND OUT MORE ABOUT OSPREY

❏ Please send me a FREE trial issue
   of Osprey Military Journal

❏ Please send me the latest listing of Osprey's publications

❏ I would like to subscribe to Osprey's e-mail newsletter

Title/rank _____

Name _____

Address _____

_____

_____

Postcode/zip _____ state/country _____

e-mail _____

Which book did this card come from?

_____

❏ I am interested in military history

My preferred period of military history is _____

❏ I am interested in military aviation

My preferred period of military aviation is _____

I am interested in (please tick all that apply)

❏ general history   ❏ militaria   ❏ model making
❏ wargaming   ❏ re-enactment

Please send to:

USA & Canada: Osprey Direct USA, c/o Motorbooks
International, P.O. Box 1, 729 Prospect Avenue, Osceola,
WI 54020

UK, Europe and rest of world:
Osprey Direct UK, P.O. Box 140, Wellingborough, Northants,
NN8 2FA, United Kingdom

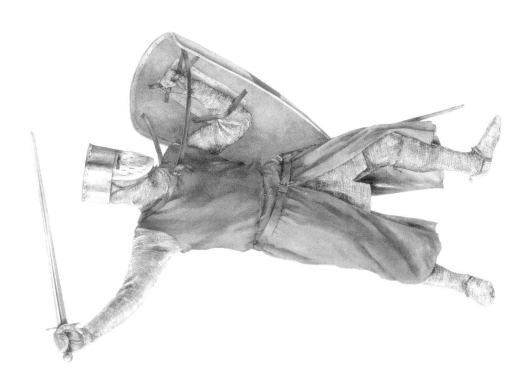

OSPREY
PUBLISHING

www.ospreypublishing.com

call our telephone hotline
for a free information pack

USA & Canada: 1-800-458-0454
UK, Europe and rest of world call:
+44 (0) 1933 443 863

Young Guardsman
Figure taken from *Warrior 22:
Imperial Guardsman 1799–1815*
Published by Osprey
Illustrated by Richard Hook

Knight, c.1190
Figure taken from *Warrior 1: Norman Knight 950 – 1204AD*
Published by Osprey
Illustrated by Christa Hook

POSTCARD